THE GOSPEL OF CHRISTIAN ATHEISM

By *Thomas J. J. Altizer*

THE GOSPEL
OF
CHRISTIAN
ATHEISM

THE WESTMINSTER PRESS
Philadelphia

Scripture quotations from the Revised Standard Version of the Bible are copyright, 1946 and 1952, by the Division of Christian Education of the National Council of Churches, and are used by permission.

Acknowledgment is made for quotations from *The Portable Nietzsche*, translated by Walter Kaufmann. Copyright 1954 by The Viking Press, Inc. Reprinted by permission of The Viking Press, Inc.

Published by The Westminster Press®
Philadelphia, Pennsylvania

PRINTED IN THE UNITED STATES OF AMERICA

In Memory of My Father

Contents

Preface

THERE WOULD seem to be little doubt that we are now entering a period in which Christianity must confront the most radical challenge that it has faced since the time of its beginning. Certainly the churches are inadequately equipped to face such a challenge, and if we were forced to rely solely upon ecclesiastical Christianity to find a way to a new Christian life and witness, then we would very nearly be without hope. But there is no intrinsic reason why Christianity should be identified with its ecclesiastical expressions. Indeed, the identification of Christianity with the Christian Church may well be the major source of the troubles that now beset the Christian faith. This study has chosen to challenge this identification, and to do so with the conviction that there is no other way to a living and contemporary Christian faith. Few Protestants are aware of how much of our inherited Christian faith and witness has its source in an increasingly archaic ecclesiastical tradition, and even fewer theologians are willing to negate all those ecclesiastical norms and traditions which are incompatible with the contemporary life of faith. But there lies no way to a contemporary epiphany of Christ apart from a consistent and thoroughgoing transformation of the language and forms of all ecclesiastical Christianity.

A truly contemporary theology can only begin its task today by first seeking a ground outside of the given and established form of the Church. A sweeping transformation is taking place in the Church today, and even Catholic theologians are calling upon the Church to enter a post-Constantinian age, a historical era following the collapse of Christendom. Yet theology need not necessarily be bound to the life of the Church, not even to the vanguard of the Church, for theology must seek the presence of Christ in the world. The first duty of the Christian theologian is loyalty to Christ, and he must strive to open his thinking to the universal presence of Christ, to the presence of Christ in the totality of human experience. Above all, a contemporary form of theology is in quest of a contemporary form of Christ. In our situation this must mean that theology is now called to listen fully to the world, even if such a listening demands a turning away from the church's witness to Christ. At a time when Christian theology is called upon to pass through the most radical revolution in its history, the theologian must not be thwarted from his goal by a false loyalty to the authority of the Church.

In dedicating this book to the memory of my father, I intend also to include all those fathers who have played such a decisive role in my life, including, most particularly, Paul Tillich. It was while reading Tillich as an undergraduate that I was led to an acceptance of the Christian faith, and I have found that throughout my teaching and study it was Tillich who exercised the greatest theological influence upon my work. Among twentieth-century theologians, it was Tillich alone who made possible a way to a truly contemporary theology. While I have been forced to resist and oppose Tillich's theological conclusions, I do so with the conviction that they are not yet radical enough, and with the memory of Tillich's words to me that the real Tillich is the radical Tillich. Certainly, Tillich is the modern father of radical theology, and although he did not succeed in founding a Tillichian school of theology, his influence is felt at most of those points where theology is now being carried beyond its traditional limits.

My own route to theology has been through the discipline of the history of religions. My teacher was Joachim Wach, and the incredible breadth of his understanding of religion beautifully exemplifies the methodological contribution that the history of religions can make to theology. More recently, Mircea Eliade is beginning to make an impact upon theology, as Rudolf Otto did before him, and I cannot refrain from once again pointing out the debt that I continue to owe to Eliade. Moreover, I am persuaded that one of the most important sources of a new direction of theology will be a new and more critical understanding of the uniqueness of Christianity. All theological talk about a "religionless Christianity" will remain largely meaningless so long as the theologian remains ignorant of the historical phenomenon of religion.

Let me confess that this book was written with the conviction that it is an expression of a new and profoundly radical theological movement in America. I have benefited immensely from the compassionate support, the patient understanding, and the probing criticism of one of my comrades-in-arms in this movement, William Hamilton, and I am more specifically indebted to him for having initiated me into the possibility of a consistent kenotic Christology. Many of my colleagues at Emory University, particularly William Mallard, have freely given me both the challenge of their criticism and the sustenance of their support, and I am indebted to Hendrikus Boers for inspiring me with the title of this book. Last fall I attended an alumni conference in the history of religions at the Divinity School of the University of Chicago, where I presented much of the material in the first chapter. This provided me with an excellent scholarly sounding board upon which to test my conception of the uniqueness of Christianity, and I am grateful for the criticism that I received from Charles H. Long, and for the ruthless way Charles

Adams forced me to revise my inadequate conception of
Islam, thus ironically allowing me to strengthen my conception of the uniqueness of the Christian God.

While writing this book I was again and again both
challenged and enlightened by questions and comments
which I received from students, teachers, monks, pastors,
priests, and even journalists. Their response openly testi-
fies to the radical theological fervor which now grips this
country, and it fully persuaded me that theology must
never again be enclosed within the classrooms and the
churches. I discovered that even the most abstruse theological problems can be opened up in the marketplace of
free discussion. A conference at Emory University on
"America and the Future of Theology" also provided me
with an exciting occasion upon which to realize the new
vocation of theology. But I owe a very special debt of
gratitude to those scholars and theologians who have
either written criticisms of my work or who have given
oral responses to my lectures. These include: Owen Bar-
field, Hendrikus Boers, Jack Boozer, Lon Chenutt, Alex-
ander Czegledy, John B. Cobb, Jr., John W. Dixon, Jr.,
Robert Funk, Langdon Gilkey, William Hamilton, Fred-
erick Herzog, Stanley Romaine Hopper, Bernard John-
son, Maynard Kaufmann, Sam Kean, Dow Kirkpatrick,
Charles H. Long, Allen Lacy, William Mallard, Thomas
Ogletree, Richard Rubenstein, Theodore Runyon, Gregor
Sebba, F. Joseph Smith, Thomas Trotter, James Wall,
Herbert Weisinger, and John Yungblut. I am also indebted
to Franklin H. Littell for introducing me to radical Prot-
estantism and for giving me the insight that the original
Christian heresy was the identification of the Church with
the body of Christ.

My wife, Gayle, shared with me the thinking that went
into this book, and her questions and criticisms were a
constant source of stimulation, to say nothing of the skill
with which she criticized my writing. I am also fortunate
in my editor, Roland W. Tapp, whose editorial wisdom is

surpassed only by the charity of his constant support. The administration of Emory University shielded me from a barrage of critical fire while I was finishing these pages, and I am also grateful to them for financial support of various kinds which made possible much of the research that went into the preparation of the book. Once again, Barbara Harkins has proved to be a devoted helper and an excellent typist. Finally, I cannot fail to express my apologies to those numerous correspondents whose letters I did not answer if only because I was determined to finish this book while still riding the momentum of my initial enthusiasm.

T. J. J. A.

Introduction

DOES GOD lie at the center of Christian faith and proclamation? Is the Christian Word forever inseparable from its historic ground in the existence and the power of God? Must Christian witness inevitably speak of the glory and the sovereignty of God? These are questions which faith itself is now posing to the Christian and they are questions that must be met by the Christian who dares to accept the contemporary challenge of faith. It is the thesis of this book that the Christian, and the Christian alone, can speak of ✳ God in our time; but the message the Christian is now called to proclaim is the gospel, the good news or the glad tidings, of the death of God. Few Christians have thus far been able to embrace the death of God as a redemptive event, but an acceptance of his death looms ever larger in contemporary Christian thinking, and it is unquestionably true that the greatest modern Christian revolutionaries willed the death of God with all the passion of faith. Christian theology, however, has yet to learn the language of the death of God. Yet this should not persuade us that we are here meeting an anti-Christian rebellion which is foreign to the reality of faith: for theology is a thinking response to the witness of faith, and it appears only after and not before the epiphany or the movement of the Christian Word. Now the time has come for theology openly and fully to confront the death of God, and whether or not a new form of theology will arise in response to this crisis, theology in our time can only refuse to speak of the death of God by ceasing to speak.

For many years a conspiracy of silence removed theology from our contemporary human and historical situation. The modern theologian, while recognizing that God was no longer visible in the culture, the society, and the history of a dying Christendom, was nevertheless persuaded that he was present, and present in his eternal form, in an autonomous Word of faith. Inevitably the price that had to be paid for such a choice was an isolation of faith from the concrete and present reality of human existence. Many ironies beset this strategy of retreat, not the least of which is the claim that was advanced by innumerable theologians that the Christian faith is uniquely "historical" and "existential," insofar as it is directed to the deepest and most immediate center of man's naked existence in the world. Needless to say, this center was identified as a broken existence of anxiety, guilt, and meaninglessness, and, even then, it was accepted only insofar as it compelled an "answer" from the Christian faith. Under the impact of an increasingly profane history, this "answer" simply evaporated or lost all human meaning, and theology was reduced once more to establishing faith as a haven from the emptiness and the ravages of an indifferent or hostile world. Meanwhile, theology ceased to speak in any meaningful way about the Word of faith. The language of the theologian became largely the polemical language of attack, assaulting other theologians for either the sacrifice of faith or the complete abandonment of all clarity and coherence, and even occasionally—and this much more timidly!— daring to attack the great outside world of unfaith or antifaith.

Today a new theologian is speaking in America, a theologian who is not so confident of the truth or certainty of faith, yet a theologian who is willing to discuss the meaning of faith. From the perspective of the theology of our century, the strangest thing about this new theologian is his conviction that faith should be meaningful and meaningful in the context of our world. Indeed, the very conviction that faith is eternally given or wholly autonomous is forcefully being challenged. Having come to the realization that Christian theology cannot survive apart from a dialogue with the world, it is increasingly being recognized that dialogue is a mutual encounter: faith cannot speak to the world unless it is prepared to be affected by that world with which it speaks. Moreover, the new theologian is confessing that the Word has ceased to be truly or decisively present in the established and traditional forms of faith. Certainly the older forms of faith have little meaning in our world, yet if we as Christians believe in an actually incarnate Word, then either the Word has perished or it has undergone a radical transformation. Refusing either to deny the Word or to affirm it in its traditional form, a modern and radical Christian is seeking a totally incarnate Word. When the Christian Word appears in this, its most radical form, then not only is it truly and actually present in the world, but it is present in such a way as to be real and active nowhere else. No longer can faith and the world exist in mutual isolation, neither can now be conceived as existing independently of the other; thus the radical Christian condemns all forms of faith that are disengaged with the world. A given and autonomous faith here reveals itself to be nonincarnate—and is judged to be a retreat from the life, the movement, and the process of history—with the result that faith must now abandon all claims to be isolated and autonomous, possessing a meaning or reality transcending the actuality of the world, and become instead wholly and inseparably embedded in the world.

Once and for all the Christian must abandon the idea ✳ that theology is a continual elucidation of an eternal and unchanging Word. If we were to accept the common distinction between dogma and doctrine—i.e., that dogma is an immovable deposit of faith and doctrine a particular expression of faith—then Christian theology may well be doctrinal but it must never be dogmatic. Only a dead or dying theology could rest upon the principle that the Christian Word is fully or finally present in the past, and surely no Christian could be wholly bound to the past who is open to the presence of a living or eschatological Word. We must not imagine that there is a single essence of Christianity, or an inner core of unchanging faith, or a form of faith meaning all things to all men. The Christian faith is real only insofar as it undergoes a particular human and historical expression, and we must not betray that faith by falsely believing that faith is confined to either its primitive or its past historical expressions. As one who is called to witness to the dynamic presence and the forward movement of the Word, the Christian must always be open to the transfiguring power of the Incarnate Word, knowing that the Word is in process of renewing all things, not by recalling them to their pristine form in the Beginning, but rather by making them new so that they can pass into the End. Therefore, Christian theology is a thinking response to the Word that is present upon the horizon of faith: but that horizon does not lie in the past, it lies in that future which extends into the present. Accordingly, a theology that merely speaks a word of the past is not engaged in the true task of Christian theology. Only a theology unveiling a new form of the Word, a form that is present or dawning in the immediate and contemporary life of faith, can be judged to be uniquely and authentically Christian.

Therefore, a faith that is truly open to the world can never be wholly or purely "faith." Such a faith can never identify itself with an ecclesiastical tradition or with a given doctrinal or ritual form. Nor can faith in this sense have any final assurance as to what it means to be a Christian, or what comprises the community of faith, or what are the signs of Christian witness in the world. We do know that Jesus himself repudiated the search for clear signs of the dawning Kingdom, dissolved the boundary between the righteous and the damned, and spoke of faith in a parabolic language that inverted the questions which it met. How are we to judge the signs of the Word or the Spirit in our own time? First, it is clear that if we were to confine Christian witness to those communities claiming to be churches, then we would in effect be denying the presence of an active or transfiguring Word, thereby making the judgment that the Christian Word is now lifeless and silent. Surely this is an alternative that is not open to the Christian theologian. Again, if we were to identify Christian witness with the compassionate life or the creative vision of those individuals or groups who confess themselves to be Christian, then we would be forced to concede that the Word is present in only a few diminishing fragments of our history. Perhaps the theologian will finally be driven to this judgment, but it could only proceed out of a counsel of despair, for so severely to limit the activity of the Word would be to abandon every claim to the effect that the Word is reconciling the world to itself. For the present time at least, theology must make another choice: it must accept the principle that the Word can be and is indeed present, even though it is not possible to discern any traditional signs of its activity, and despite the fact that the life and movement of our time would appear to be so irrevocably anti-Christian.

Let us assume that Christian theology is directed to the goal of unveiling that form of the Word which is present or dawning in the contemporary community of faith. What is that community? Where is it to be found? How is its language or activity to be interpreted by the theologian who knows full well that his is a time of spiritual darkness? In the past, theologians have dared to claim that nothing which is human is foreign to faith. Can we make that claim? Can we go beyond it and assert as a matter of principle that the most authentically human is a manifestation of faith? Yet all that we once knew as human is disappearing in our history, the classical Western form of the unique and autonomous person is vanishing in our midst, and we have long since ceased to have imaginative expressions or conceptual portraits of the Christian man. Perhaps we are too numbed by the horrors of the twentieth century to discern in its assaults upon an inherited form of humanity an epiphany of the Spirit. Nevertheless, we would seem by this time to have arrived at a sufficient distance from the nineteenth century to make possible a positive theological appraisal of its revolutionary achievement. Two generations of theologians have now finished their work of attacking the atheism of the nineteenth century and building upon that attack an autonomous form of the Word which is isolated from the demonic threats of a profane history. We have seen that this theological choice has finally issued in a wholly inhuman and meaningless form of the Word. May we retrace the footsteps of our elders and meet the atheism of the modern world with acceptance and affirmation? Nothing less will be required of the theologian who fully opens himself to the creative vision of the nineteenth century, for it was that vision which established the ground of contemporary atheism, and one has only to observe the dominance of atheism in our century to sense the overwhelming power and apparently inescapable consequence of the nineteenth-century prophetic proclamation that God is dead.

Once we have decided to engage in a positive theological confrontation with the nineteenth-century vision, we soon discover that even in its most atheistic expressions it is inseparable from both a strange but radical form of the Christian faith and a passionate affirmation of the birth of a new humanity. True, the world has given us no more violent anti-Christians than the nineteenth-century prophets. Their attack upon Christianity, however, was directed against those very theological forms and moral laws which they knew to be most opposed to the advent of a new man. It is also significant to observe that these atheistic prophets venerated Jesus, were fully persuaded that the Christian tradition had either buried or inverted both his message and his person, and frequently invoked either the name of Jesus or the Christian symbol of the Incarnate Word to sanction their most radical proclamation. Moreover, it would not be unjust to say that these prophets were obsessed with Christianity—here they differ all too clearly from their twentieth-century descendants—and this obsession cannot be explained merely by noting the still lingering power of the Christian tradition in their time, for most of these prophets again and again return to their struggle with Christianity both in their most private writings and in their greatest imaginative and conceptual achievements. If even a violently hostile passion is a measure of attachment, then who can doubt that a Blake, a Hegel, a Marx, a Dostoevsky, and a Nietzsche were deeply bound to Christianity? Again, each of these prophets was motivated by a profound moral passion—and despite appearances to the contrary, this is no less true of Hegel—which, although it assumed an antinomian form, must surely have had its roots in the prophetic traditions of Christianity and the Bible. Indeed, these greatest and most radical creators of modern atheism have ironically proved to be the most seminal influence upon twentieth-century Christian thinking.

No graver charge has ever been leveled against Christianity than the typically modern protest that the Christian faith is a flight from life, an evasion of suffering, a refusal of the burden and the anguish of the human condition. Nietzsche's symbol of "No-saying" may be taken as epitomizing the condemnation of Christianity that has become dominant in the modern world. As Nietzsche said in *The Antichrist:*

> The Christian conception of God—God as god of the sick, God as a spider, God as spirit—is one of the most corrupt conceptions of the divine ever attained on earth. It may even represent the low-water mark in the descending development of divine types. God degenerated into the *contradiction* of life, instead of being its transfigura-

tion and eternal Yes! God as the declaration of war against life, against nature, against the will to live! God—the formula for every slander against "this world," for every lie about the "beyond"! God—the deification of nothingness, the will to nothingness pronounced holy! (Section 18.)

Unlike the far weaker contemporary attacks of a Lawrence or a Camus, Nietzsche's protest against Christianity, like Blake's and Hegel's, is most fundamentally directed against the Christian God. It is God himself who is the transcendent enemy of the fullness and the passion of man's life in the world, and only through God's death can humanity be liberated from that repression which is the real ruler of history. Standing upon the threshold of what he believed to be a new age of humanity, the nineteenth-century prophet identified the God of Christianity as the deepest obstacle to liberty and joy. Blake gradually came to the realization that the true name of the Christian God is Satan, just as Hegel conceived of the "false infinite" or the impassive and unmoving Absolute as the ultimate source of alienation, and Nietzsche disclosed God to be the very embodiment of an infinitude of man's self-hatred and guilt. Thus the triumphant Blake could say in *The Everlasting Gospel:* "Thou are a Man, God is no more."

If there is one clear portal to the twentieth century, it is a passage through the death of God, the collapse of any meaning or reality lying beyond the newly discovered radical immanence of modern man, an immanence dissolving even the memory or the shadow of transcendence. With that collapse has come a new chaos, a new meaninglessness brought on by the disappearance of an absolute or transcendent ground, the very nihilism foreseen by Nietzsche as the next stage of history. Just as ancient myths of creation envision a repetition of creation by way of a return to the primordial chaos, and religious rites of initiation effect a symbolic passage through death, the new humanity lying upon our horizon can be reached only by means of a voyage through that darkness which has fallen with the breakdown of our past.

Must the contemporary Christian refuse the dark chaos of our time? Is our faith a lifeline to the submerged roots of a vanished Christendom? Can we believe that the Christian alone among men in our day possesses the assurance that can give meaning and direction to life? Is only the Christian to be spared the broken condition of a life without roots? Must we join the modern atheist in declaring that Christianity is a flight from this world to the beyond? Certainly, few responsible Christians would answer these questions affirmatively, but we must recognize that to cling to the Christian God in our time is to evade the human situation of our century and to renounce the inevitable suffering which is its lot. Already a Kierkegaard and a Dostoevsky knew that no suffering can be foreign to the Christian, not even the anguish that comes with the loss of God, for the way of the Christian is to bear with Jesus all the pain of the flesh.

In the perspective of the atheistic historical destiny of our time, a time in which simply to share the universal condition of man is to take upon oneself a life without God, it does not seem amiss to pose the problem of the necessity of a contemporary Christian atheism. This study has accepted this necessity by way of constructing a theological analysis based upon the Christian visions of Blake, Hegel, and Nietzsche. But in what sense may we think of these revolutionary figures as Christian prophets? There is a substantial body of scholarly analysis in agreement with the judgment that Blake was a Christian visionary and Hegel a Christian thinker, but they remain untapped sources for the theologian. The question of Nietzsche would appear to be far simpler, for there is virtually a unanimous scholarly concurrence with Nietzsche's own self-judgment that he was a profoundly anti-Christian thinker, and the theologian has employed Nietzsche only to point to the antithesis of faith. Yet it cannot be acci-

dental that so many of the more creative theologians of
our century have implicitly if unconsciously shared much
of Nietzsche's vision—e.g., the early Barth, Bultmann,
Tillich, and the late Bonhoeffer—and it would be difficult
to deny the fact that Nietzsche's whole vision evolved out
of what he himself proclaimed to be the death of the Christian God, and we shall attempt to show that this event can
only be perceived by faith. Although it is understandable
why twentieth-century theology thus far at least should
have openly set itself against Nietzsche, it seems strange
that Blake should be unknown to the theologian and Hegel
commonly regarded, following Kierkegaard's judgment,
as being an enemy of faith (few theologians have taken
account of the fact that Kierkegaard adapted almost the
whole movement and method of his thought from Hegel).
Can it have no theological significance that Blake is the
most Christocentric of all poets and Hegel the only thinker
who made the kenotic movement of the Incarnation the
core and foundation of all his thinking? Or has the theologian recognized that an acceptance of Blake or Hegel
would demand a revolutionary transformation of Christian
language and theology?

However, it must be confessed that we can by no means
think even of Blake as a Christian visionary unless we are
prepared to give a new theological status to the radical
Christian. Inasmuch as radical Christianity has never made
a real impact upon theology, and has only once—in the
work of William Blake—been given a full imaginative expression, theology at present has neither the methods nor
the categories to make possible a theological understanding of a Blake or a Hegel. Church historians have been
so delinquent—or so bound to the churches—that it is not
even possible to piece together the full and continuing history of radical Christianity, although we know that it is
present in many forms of Christian mysticism as well as in
numerous sects. Nor can we fail to observe that Blake
shares many of the motifs of the seventeenth-century radi-

cal English Protestants: an antinomian ethics, a violent rebellion against both the Christian tradition and the Christian churches, and a belief only in the spiritual Jesus of the third and apocalyptic age of the Spirit. Renouncing both cult and doctrine, the radical Christian seeks a total union with Jesus or the Word, and repudiates the God who is the sovereign Creator and the transcendent Lord (and this rebellion against the Christian God may be seen in a philosophical form in Whitehead as well as in Hegel). It is this passionate protest against the Christian God that is both strange and offensive to the common Christian, but to the radical Christian there is no way to true faith apart from an abolition or dissolution of God himself. Once we recognize that radical Christianity is inseparable from an attack upon God, then we should be prepared to face the possibility that even Nietzsche was a radical Christian.

Now, what can it mean to seek a radical form of Christian theology or a form of Christian language reflecting and embodying the vision of the modern atheistic Christian prophet? First, it is all too clear that such a language must set itself against the Christian tradition, not simply by way of negating its doctrinal and ritual forms but, rather, by inverting its forms and structures so as to reverse that history revolving about the epiphany of the Christian God. Radical Christians are Protestants insofar as they seek a return to the original Word of faith. But recognizing the reality of the process of history, and the forward movement of Word and Spirit, they are in quest of a renewal of the original Jesus in the spiritual or universal form demanded by the apocalyptic or final age of the Spirit. No radical Christian believes in the possibility of returning to either the word or the person of the original Jesus of Nazareth. Consequently, the radical Christian rejects both the literal and the historical interpretation of the Bible, demanding instead a pneumatic or spiritual understanding of the Word. Above all, the radical Christian seeks a total union with the Word, a union abolishing the priestly, legalistic, and dogmatic norms of the churches, so as to make possible the realization of a total redemption, a redemption actualizing the eschatological promise of Jesus. It is this quest for total redemption—and nothing has so violently aroused the theological spokesmen of the churches—that demands the death of the Christian God, the God who is the sovereign Lord and almighty Creator. The radical Christian must not be thought of as a reformer; he believes that the ecclesiastical tradition has ceased to be Christian, and is now alive only in a demonic and repressive form. No, the radical Christian is a revolutionary, he is given to a total transformation of Christianity, a rebirth of the Christian Word in a new and final form.

The Church has ceased to be Christian

There can be no doubt that any attempt to give expression in theological language to the radical Christian vision demands a thorough rethinking of the meaning of faith. Although all original Christian thinking has been radical insofar as it effected a transformation of an inherited theological language—e.g., Paul, the author of the Gospel of John, Augustine, Luther, and Kierkegaard—theology has never before been called upon to effect or record a total transformation of faith. Fortunately, it is not necessary for the theologian to create a new language of faith; this has in large measure been accomplished by the Christian revolutionaries of the nineteenth century. Nevertheless, it is necessary for the theologian to mediate the radical Christian vision to the forms of theological discourse. Just as the postexilic Jewish scribes and priests evolved a new religious form as a means of giving expression to the radical faith of the preexilic and exilic prophets, so the Christian theologian must now formulate a theological language that will capture the radical faith of the modern Christian prophets. If Israel through the exile lost very nearly everything that was the source of meaning and order to an ancient people, so Christianity today is passing through an exile from Christendom, an exile demanding a rebirth and

Need for a new language for faith

reconstruction that is every bit as thoroughgoing as that
effected by postexilic Judaism. The contemporary theo-   ✻
logian should not imagine that he is simply the servant of
an ancient faith and cultus, for that faith and cultus has
almost disappeared from view, and to identify theology
with a backward quest for the past is to foreclose the possibility of a truly Christian theology that is a response to
the movement of the Word in the present.

Perhaps the deepest obstacle to the realization of this   ✻
new vocation of theology is the priestly conviction that the
canon of Scripture is closed, revelation is finished and   *Closed*
complete, the Word of God has already been fully and   *revelation*
finally spoken. Later we shall raise the question as to
whether this belief is possible for the Christian; but already   *the*
Paul could only establish his apostleship by insisting upon   *enemy*
his own immediate communion with the Word, and Paul's   *of*
Word, like the radical Christian's, demands an annulment
of the old covenant of Sinai and the Torah of Israel's   *theological*
priestly and legal traditions. The radical Christian also in-   *advance.*
herits both the ancient prophetic belief that revelation continues in history and the eschatological belief of the tradition following Joachim of Floris. This tradition maintains
that we are now living in the third and final age of the   *Opts*
Spirit, that a new revelation is breaking into this age, and   *strongly*
that this revelation will differ as much from the New Testa-   *for*
ment as the New Testament itself does from its Old Testa-   *continu-*
ment counterpart. Of course, the great Christian revolutionaries of the nineteenth century went far beyond their   *ing*
spiritual predecessors. But we can learn from earlier radi-   *revelat-*
cal Christians the root radical principle that the movement   *ion.*
of the Spirit has passed beyond the revelation of the ca-
nonical Bible and is now revealing itself in such a way as
to demand a whole new form of faith. To refuse such a
new revelation of the Spirit would be to repudiate the activity of the Word which is present and to bind oneself to
a now empty and lifeless form of the Word. Nor can we expect the new revelation to be in apparent continuity with

the old. Now that historical scholarship has demonstrated the chasm existing between the Old Testament and the Christian visions of Paul and the Gospel of John, might we not expect a comparable chasm to exist between the New Testament and a new revelation? Yet this should by no means persuade us that no new revelation has occurred. We can only judge by the fruits of the Spirit, and if a new vision has arisen recording a universal and eschatological form of the Word, a form of the Word pointing to a total redemption of history and the cosmos, then we should be prepared to greet it with the full acceptance of faith.

The risk
— Loss
of Faith.

Let us openly confess that a Christian who embarks upon a quest of this order is not only voyaging into a strange new country but is also submitting himself to the hazard of an irretrievable loss of faith. Again and again Christian theologians have told us that faith is a risk— despite the fact that few theologians have ventured to take upon themselves anything more than a token risk—and we must recognize that a faith which is not open to the loss of faith is not a true form of faith. A faith that is a haven from doubt and suffering is not only a false faith but is a reversal of the kenotic way of the Word. More- over, the Christian can only participate in the suffering and broken body of the humanity of our time by freely sharing the depths of its anguish and despair, not with the self-conscious realization that his participation is vicarious, but rather with the certainty that there is no true suffering which is foreign to faith. If ours is a time that shatters the very possibility of faith, then the Christian faith is in vain, and the honest man can only renounce all faith. Therefore, for those Christians who have discovered that an estab- lished form of faith has become wholly unreal, there is really no choice, we must either open ourselves to a new form of faith or abandon faith itself. Few will follow the way that this book has chosen, but if it but points a way to the renewal of faith, it will have succeeded in its purpose.

Bibliographical Note

THE PRIMARY sources of this book are the writings of
Blake, Hegel, and Nietzsche. A word of warning is in order
about the punctuation of the Blake quotations. Blake himself employed little punctuation, and the punctuation in
the citations here is simply taken verbatim from Sir
Geoffrey Keynes's 1957 edition of the *Complete Writings
of William Blake* (Random House, Inc.). However,
David V. Erdman and Harold Bloom have just published
the most critical edition yet of Blake's poetry and prose,
attempting to preserve the original state of his texts (Dou-
bleday & Company, Inc., 1965). My citations from Hegel
are taken from J. B. Baillie's translation of *The Phenomenology of the Mind* (The Macmillan Company, 1949)
and from W. H. Johnston's and L. G. Struthers' translation
of the *Science of Logic* (The Macmillan Company, 1952).
The quotations of *Thus Spoke Zarathustra* and *The Antichrist* are taken from the translations of Walter Kaufmann
as contained in *The Viking Portable Nietzsche* (The Viking Press, Inc., 1954). Let me add that my interpretation
of Blake has been most affected by the studies of Northrup
Frye and Joseph Wicksteed, and that my understanding of
Hegel has been reached in part by way of the studies of
John Findlay, Karl Löwith, and Herbert Marcuse.

I

The Uniqueness of Christianity

I. RELIGION

AN IRONIC dilemma of contemporary theology derives from its increasing insistence that Christianity both transcends and negates religion even while theology refuses to open itself to an understanding of the actual nature or the historical phenomenon of religion. The persistent calls for a "religionless Christianity" can have little meaning so long as religion is conceived of as merely a false righteousness or a shallow piety. All too clearly such conceptions of religion are reflections of the lifeless body of a dying Christendom, and while ultimately they may well derive from the historical actualization of Kierkegaard's prophetic judgment that the Christianity of the New Testament no longer exists, it is nevertheless true that the problem of the relation between Christianity and religion has now become both inescapable and overwhelming. Immediately we must recognize that this problem has a historical ground: Christianity is losing its ancient body; no longer can it find life in its traditional form, and to the extent that it speaks its former language its witness becomes empty and silent. Faith must now find a trans-Christian language—i.e., a language substantially if not wholly different from its previous speech—if it is to exist and to live as faith. Not only must it abandon its own language, but it must likewise move beyond all that meaning which Christianity once shared with the universal community of belief.

[margin handwritten note: The forms of Christianity no longer express the living truth of faith.]

Despite the fact that the last two hundred years has seen the birth and the flowering of the historical discipline of the history of religions, the historian of religions has not been notably successful in meeting the problem of the uniqueness of Christianity. Few Christians doubt the genuine distinctiveness of Christianity, but this distinctiveness has for the most part been formulated in terms adapted from the general culture of Christendom, and that culture is now in process of disintegration or transformation, thereby leading to the bankruptcy of the established conceptions of the unique and particular nature of the Christian faith. Strangely enough, the theologian has had little interest in the relation between Christianity and the non-Christian religions, largely confining himself to extravagant claims bearing little relationship to the non-Christian religious world. If only because Christian theology has for the most part attempted to establish an impassable gulf between Christianity and the non-Christian religions, it would seem that an elucidation of the genuine and full uniqueness of Christianity might unveil its deepest faith; but this is a challenge which continues to go unanswered. Moreover this challenge cannot be met apart from a confrontation of Christianity with the highest expressions of religion. Of course, there are higher forms of religion that seemingly resist all comparisons with Christianity—the Olympian religion of ancient Greece and the Confucian tradition of the Far East quickly come to mind—just as Judaism and Islam are so close to the religious form of Christianity that they can scarcely provide the necessary perspective for an assessment of the full distinctiveness of the Christian faith. It is, rather, in the purer forms of Oriental mysticism that the Christian theologian must seek out the deepest challenge of the non-Christian religious world.

Obviously this study can do no more than make certain general observations about the relationship between Christianity and Oriental mysticism, and these observations will bear little historical or scholarly authority, but they are nonetheless deemed essential to our theological goal. If we can point to a root and fundamental difference between Christianity and the forms of Oriental mysticism, then this difference will have a significant bearing upon the problem of the authentic meaning of the Christian faith, and can serve as a basis for a liberation of Christianity from an inessential and now archaic religious form. We must first arrive at some sense of what these various mystical forms have in common, assuming that here we do indeed find a true manifestation of religion. Granted that any effort to capture the common form of such an exceedingly complex phenomenon as Oriental mysticism will lose much of its richness and power, this is a price which must be paid for our own particular purpose. Inevitably we must also view Oriental mysticism from the vantage point of our own historical situation, confessing that it will have meaning to us only from our own point of view, even if such a perspective must necessarily lead to what the Oriental religious mind would judge to be a false conception. Yet by choosing the higher expressions of the Oriental religious vision as the arena in which to confront Christianity with the non-Christian religions, we may safely assume that we are taking up the full challenge of our problem.

Our initial judgment about Oriental mysticism must be that it is a way of radical world-negation. Directing itself against the ordinary contents of consciousness and all those forms of experience and perception resulting from an individual self's encounter with both the interior and the exterior worlds, this is a form of religion seeking an absolute negation of the immediate and actual reality that is manifest in the world. Oriental mysticism sets itself against the autonomy of that which appears before it, seizing upon the actuality of that which happens to exist or to be at hand as the initial springboard for its own movement of negation. However, this movement of radical negation is inseparable from an interior recovery of a sacred Totality, a primordial Totality embodying in a unified form all those antinomies that have created an alienated and estranged existence. Transcending the mythical and ritual forms of a communal and cultic religion, the higher expressions of mysticism in the Orient culminate in an interior epiphany of the primordial Totality. Whether this Totality is symbolically known as Brahman-Atman, Nirvana, Tao, or Sunyata, it always becomes manifest in a mystical form as the original identity of an unfallen cosmos. Yet the primordial Totality, which is known here as ultimate Reality, can only appear and be real to the mystic by means of an absolute and total negation of the fallen forms of the world. True, Eastern ways of negation differ substantially from one another; a difference particularly to be noted between the gradual way of the various forms of Indian Yoga and the spontaneous and immediate way of Taoism and Zen. So likewise the form of the negation differs insofar as these are distinct and singular mystical ways, leading to widely different apprehensions of the relation between an original Totality and the fallen or apparent forms of the world. Nevertheless, it remains true that the Oriental mystic can only reach his goal of total redemption by means of a radical negation of *all* that reality which is present to an individual and isolated human consciousness.

Now, despite those critics who insist that this negative movement of Oriental mysticism sets it wholly apart from the prophetic faith of the Bible or the Judeo-Christian-Islamic tradition, we must recognize that all expressions of religion in some measure share such a movement of negation. Religion must necessarily direct itself against a selfhood, a history, or a cosmos existing immediately and autonomously as its own creation or ground. Thus Hegel believed that religion is identical with dialectical or true philosophical understanding insofar as both must negate the Given: "For religion equally with philosophy refuses to recognize in finitude a veritable being, or something

ultimate and absolute, or non-posited, uncreated, and
eternal" (*Logic,* Vol. I, Bk. I, Ch. 3). We might also note
that critical definitions of religion in all their variety show
that the sacred or the religious life is the opposite of the
profane and the secular life. What is important from our
Christian point of view is to realize that the negative movement of Oriental mysticism is a *backward* movement to
the primordial Totality. The Oriental mystic, whether
Hindu or Buddhist, Far Eastern or Indian, reverses ordinary life and consciousness so as to make possible a return
to the paradisical Beginning. He seeks a repetition of an
original paradise in the present moment, a repetition effecting an absolute reversal of a fallen or profane reality,
and moving whether suddenly or gradually through a total
inversion of the concrete processes of time and history.
Remembering that Kierkegaard identified recollection as
the pagan life view, we might conceive the negative movement of Oriental mysticism as a process of involution.
Here the mystic reverses the fallen order of history and
the cosmos so as to return to an unfallen Beginning.
Whereas the prophetic faith of the Old Testament and the
primitive faith of Christianity were directed to a future
and final End, and thus are inseparable from a forward-
moving and eschatological ground, the multiple forms of
Oriental mysticism revolve about a backward movement
to the primordial Totality, a process of cosmic and historical involution wherein all things return to their pristine
form.

The Westerner would be grievously misled if he were
to think that the backward movement of Oriental mysticism is confined to Eastern religion and occupies no role
in the religious forms of his own tradition. Very nearly
all forms of cultic or priestly religion, including those of
Judaism and Christianity, revolve about a concrete renewal
or a representation (*anamnēsis*) of a sacred time of the
past. We should, rather, think of Oriental mysticism as
bringing to its purest and most interior expression a move-

ment of reversal and return that is universally present in religion. Moreover, it is of vital importance to realize that when this negative movement of return achieves its highest expression in Oriental mysticism, it is indissolubly linked with an apprehension of the sacred as an original or primordial Reality. If only because the Oriental mystic carries this religious way of involution and reversal to its radical and inevitable conclusion, he reaches the final goal of a backward movement of return: the original and unfallen Totality of the Beginning. Accordingly, the higher Oriental symbols of the sacred give witness to an eternal, an inactive, or a quiescent Totality, and a Totality that only truly appears with the disappearance or inactivity of all motion and process. Just as this very *dis*appearance or *in*activity repeats or resurrects the original Totality, it could even be said that the Oriental mystic must understand the advent of motion and process to be the beginning of the Fall, despite the fact that here neither motion nor process can be judged to be ultimately or finally real. Underlying all forms of Oriental mysticism is a cosmic and interior process of regeneration, a fully mystical process that either annuls or dissolves both spatial location and temporal duration, leading to the epiphany of a precosmic or pretemporal Totality. Hence, the Oriental seer invariably speaks of this Totality as a timeless Eternity, a Nothing, or a Void.

Too frequently we Westerners attempt to translate the symbols of Oriental religion into the language of our own Western ontology. Whereas the Western thinker has an almost invariable tendency to place a positive and even absolute evaluation upon existence and being, the Eastern mystical thinker begins with the conviction that actual or existing being must be abolished or reversed to make possible an epiphany of Being. Both the Chinese and the Indian Buddhists paradoxically employ words whose immediate and literal reference is to nonbeing and to nothingness when they wish to speak of ultimate Reality. So likewise we cannot understand the Hindu symbols Brahman and Sat if we imagine them to represent a Being existing in continuity with the world of actuality. The language of Oriental mysticism is consistently and fully dialectical: it can speak of the sacred only by inverting the meaning of the profane, and its symbols of the sacred always refer to a total dissolution or reversal of an actual and immediately existent being. Finally, the language of the Oriental mystic is the language of silence. He can speak only by inverting or reversing all common and established meaning. But this practice must culminate in the cessation of speech. Total silence is the only appropriate witness to an absolutely quiescent Totality, just as the mystic who embraces this highest of religious ways must finally abandon all symbols, all language, all discipline, and all meaning. Why should the Oriental mystic concern himself with language when finally he knows that the truest communication takes place by way of silence? Such silence is beyond all possibility of realization wherever there is the presence of action, movement, or process. Thus here lies the necessity for mystical ways to abolish all actual or willful movement, whether by way of the *wu wei* or inaction of Taoism and Zen, or the Yogic discipline of emptying the contents of consciousness, or even the purposeless action of the Bhagavad-Gita. All such ways finally carry the mystic to that total quiescence which is an absolute inversion of everything that the Western ontological tradition has known as Being.

It is precisely because the Oriental mystical way revolves about a negation of all that reality which the Western mind knows as Being that it must appear to us as a way of radical world-negation. Yet Oriental mysticism, like all the highest expressions of religion, whether in East or West, follows a dialectical way. It seeks a total negation of the "being" that is manifest in the world as a means of transforming time into Eternity or of unveiling the fallen form of the world as the elusive mask of an unfallen Totality. Here, in the higher forms of Oriental religion, what

The
Oriental
form of
negation
is simply
a backwards
march
toward
the divine.

would appear to us to be a simple negation of the world is at bottom an epiphany, a renewal, or a repetition of the Totality of the Beginning. Dialectically, an absolute negation of the profane is identical with a total affirmation of the sacred. Consequently, the symbol of the *coincidentia oppositorum* lies at the center of Oriental mysticism. All too naturally we employ a Latin phrase in speaking of the "coincidence of the opposites." For it is none too clear as to whether *coincidentia* is a coincidence, a harmony, a unity, or an identity of the opposites. But with this ambiguity the meaning of the opposites themselves is obscured; and we cannot arrive at a theological understanding of Oriental mysticism so long as we remain unclear as to the opposition that it initially posits, and then finally removes, between the sacred and the profane. What is that "being" whose absolute negation issues in an epiphany of a cosmic Totality? What meaning can we give to a seemingly fallen profane reality that the mystic ultimately comes to know as total bliss? How can a world that is judged to be an arena of turbulence and suffering finally become manifest in a wholly sacred form as absolute Quiescence?

Certainly the Oriental mystic reaches his goal of absolute Quiescence by means of an inversion of human consciousness and a corresponding reversal of the cosmos. However, when the negative movement of religion is wholly a reversal of the profane, acting by way of a backward movement or return, the sacred must inevitably appear as an original or primordial Reality. It is the total repetition of this primordial Totality which reveals the sacred identity of the profane. We might even say that a purely mystical repetition annuls the possibility of profane existence, reversing its form and structure so as to make possible its manifestation as the original sacred, thereby definitively and finally abolishing the profane or fallen form of the world. Therefore a *coincidentia oppositorum* in this sense must identify the opposites by abolishing their opposition—an abolition effected by an absolute negation of the profane—and here *coincidentia* must finally mean a nondialectical "identity." If by one means or another all forms of Oriental mysticism culminate in an identification of *nirvana* and *samsara,* then this is an identity in which the opposition between the sacred and the profane has wholly disappeared. No longer does either the sacred or the profane bear a polar or dialectical meaning, for with the abolition of the profane consciousness all human or worldly meaning has vanished. Now silence reigns triumphant, an absolute Quiescence has become all in all, the sacred has returned to its original form, and thus it ceases to exist in opposition to the profane. When the Oriental mystic insists that ultimately the "way" of mysticism must be abandoned, he is speaking of a transcendence of religion, a transcendence of the movement of dialectical negation. His goal is the cessation of all movement and process, including the movement of religion, and with the realization of that goal every individual identity returns to its primordial source.

May we allow this understanding of Oriental mysticism to represent the true meaning of the negative or mystical movement of religion? Granted that it does violence to the complex historical phenomena of the higher religions of the Orient, does it apprehend a meaning of the ground of religion that is relevant to the contemporary Christian goal of the negation of religion? If religion is understood to be a backward movement of return to an original sacred, does this give us a proper basis for assessing the uniqueness of Christianity? Surely it gives us insight into the presence of universal religious forms within the historical body of Christianity: a nostalgia for a lost paradise, a quest for an original innocence, a cultic re-presentation or recollection of a sacred history of the past, a conception of faith as contemporaneity with an ancient or long distant epiphany of Christ, a belief in a primordial God whose very sacrality annuls or negates the existence of the profane, and a longing for an eschatological End that will be a repetition of the primordial Beginning. At all these points and others we find religious forms within Christianity that belie its claim to uniqueness. Assuming that the true center of Christianity nevertheless remains unique, what is the relation of that center to these universal religious forms? Can it fully appear or become truly manifest apart from a negation or transcendence of these forms? The call for a "religionless Christianity" can mean no less than this, nor can it have real meaning apart from a resolution to abandon the whole religious body of Christianity, even if that body should prove to comprehend very nearly everything which Christianity once knew as faith. Above all, a reborn and radical Christian faith must renounce every temptation to return to an original or primordial sacred, or to follow a backward path leading to an earlier and presumably purer form of the Word, or to seek a total silence in which both Word and world will have disappeared.

II. WORD AND HISTORY

Having seen that a pure form of religion knows the sacred as an original, an immobile, and an impassive reality, can we conceive the uniqueness of the Christian Word to lie in the fact that it is a dynamic, a living, and a forward-moving process? It is seldom remarked that theology, in its distinctively Christian form, is a unique creation of Christianity. Christian theology is a thinking response to the Word that is actively present upon the horizon of faith, and thus it is neither a systematization of a mythical vision nor a metaphysical or mystical system. The Christian Word appears in neither a primordial nor an eternal form: for it is an incarnate Word, a Word that is real only to the extent that it becomes one with human flesh. If we are to preserve the uniqueness of the Christian Word, we cannot understand the Incarnation as a final and once-and-for-all event of the past. On the contrary, the Incarnation must be conceived as an active and forward-moving process, a process that even now is making all things new. Unless we are prepared to allow the Christian Word to recede into an impassive and primordial form, we must acknowledge its occurrence in the present, no matter what form that present may assume to the believing consciousness of faith. There are times, and certainly ours is not the least of them, when the darkness of history would seem to impel faith to seek an earlier and even primordial form of the Word. Then theology is tempted to conceive the Word in an abstract, an inhuman, and a nonhistorical form. Yet we must confess this to be an anti-Christian temptation if we are not to succumb to a regressive and backward movement of the religious form of faith, a form that ever threatens a true witness to the Incarnation.

Christian theologians and historians of religion are united in asserting that the uniqueness of Christianity derives from its proclamation of the Incarnation; thus Archbishop Söderblom has judged that uniqueness to lie in the fact that here revelation has the form of a "man." However, a movement of incarnation, of the transition of Spirit into flesh, is not unique to Christianity. Already we have observed an act of repetition in Oriental religion in which flesh is transformed into Spirit in such a way that flesh loses its own apparently intrinsic form and Spirit ceases to exist in opposition to flesh. What is distinctive to Christianity is a witness to an incarnation in which Spirit becomes flesh in such a manner as to continue to exist and to act as flesh. Such a movement is both active and real, because here we do not find an unveiling of the illusory form of flesh, but rather an actual movement of Spirit's decisively and truly becoming flesh. Christian theology has never thought through the full meaning of the Incarnation if only because it has remained bound to an eternal and primordial form of Spirit. When Spirit is apprehended in this religious form, it obviously can never be known as becoming fully incarnate, and thus the Christian doctrine of the Incarnation has thus far only been able to posit a Word that is partially flesh and partially Spirit. Despite the Nicene formula, the Word cannot be fully God and fully man if, on the one hand, it continues to exist in an eternal form and, on the other, it is unable to move into the present and the full reality of history.

Throughout its history Christian theology has been thwarted from reaching its intrinsic goal by its bondage to a transcendent, a sovereign, and an impassive God. Once having absorbed a Greek metaphysical idea of God as an eternal and unmoving Being, and having refused Paul's proclamation of faith as freedom from a moral law and a priestly cultus, Christian theology found its ground in the God who alone is God, the awesome Creator and the distant Lord. No way lay from this transcendent and wholly other God to the Incarnation, the act of the Word's becoming flesh, apart from a transformation of the Incarnate Word into an eternal Logos and a mysterious Lord. Blake's Albion, a symbolic figure representing a cosmic and universal Humanity, while dying under the weight of sin and darkness, curses the Christian God—"God in the dreary Void dwells from Eternity, wide separated from the Human Soul"—and then he laments the disappearance of the merciful Lamb of God:

> O Human Imagination, O Divine Body I have Crucified,
> I have turned my back upon thee into the Wastes of Moral Law.
> There Babylon is builded in the Waste, founded in Human desolation.
>
> . . . .
>
> The footsteps of the Lamb of God were there; but now no more,
> No more shall I behold him; he is clos'd in Luvah's Sepulcher.
>
> (*Jerusalem* 24:23-51.)

Luvah's sepulcher, most simply interpreted, is the repressive body of the Christian Church—as Nietzsche remarked, Christianity is the stone upon the grave of Jesus —for Blake, like many radical Christians before him, believed that the resurrected Lord was an epiphany of the wholly other God who had been left behind by the movement of the Incarnation. Like the Krishna who appears to Arjuna in the Bhagavad-Gita, the resurrected Christ of Christianity is a monarchic Lord and cosmic Logos. Despite the efforts of modern theologians to formulate a kenotic Christology, a doctrine of the incarnate Lord as a consequence of the emptying of the power of God, an understanding of a fully kenotic Christ continues to elude the theologian, who at best has reached Karl Barth's ironic and antikenotic conclusion that God's omnipotence is such that it can assume the form of weakness and in that form can triumph.

The problem that the theologian refuses to confront is the inevitable incompatability between the primordial Christian God and an incarnate or kenotic Christ, a refusal arising from a new epiphany of the primordial Godhead in Christian history. Even as Christianity almost immediately came to worship Christ in the image of the Hellenistic mystery gods, the Christ of Christianity has almost invariably appeared in the form of a high god or heavenly deity which is found almost everywhere in the history of religions. Certainly the Christ who is fully God is not unique to Christianity, except insofar as he bears some sign of a concrete descent of God into human flesh. Such a descent cannot be truly meaningful unless it is understood as a real movement of God himself, a movement which is final and irrevocable, but which continues to occur wherever there is history and life. So long as the Christian God continues to be known as transcendent and impassive, or as a primordial deity who is unaffected by the processes of time and history, he cannot appear in his uniquely Christian form as the Incarnate Word and the kenotic Christ. Thus the radical Christian reverses the orthodox confession, affirming that "God is Jesus" (Blake's Laocoön engraving), rather than "Jesus is God." Before the Incarnation can be understood as a decisive and real event, it must be known as effecting a real change or movement in God himself: God becomes incarnate in the Word, and he becomes fully incarnate, thereby ceasing to exist or to be present in his primordial form. To say that "God is Jesus" is to say that God has become the Incarnate Word, he has abandoned or negated his transcendent form; or, rather, he remains present and real in his original form only where faith itself refuses to become incarnate.

A religious form of Christianity resists this forward movement of the Incarnation, regressing to a preincarnate form of the Word, and by this means dualistically isolating flesh from Spirit. Only in radical Christianity do we find a fulfillment of the incarnate movement of the Christian Word, and here alone do we discover a "religionless Christianity." The radical Christian identifies religion with a repressive opposition to the Word of life because in its Christian form it effects a reversal of the Incarnation. Thus Blake prophetically denounces natural religion in his address, "To the Christians," in *Jerusalem:*

> I stood among my valleys of the south
> And saw a flame of fire, even as a Wheel
> Of fire surrounding all the heavens: it went
> From west to east, against the current of
> Creation, and devour'd all things in its loud
> Fury & thundering course round heaven & earth.
> By it the Sun was roll'd into an orb,
> By it the Moon faded into a globe
> Travelling thro' the night; for, from its dire
> And restless fury, Man himself shrunk up
> Into a little root a fathom long.
> And I asked a Watcher & a Holy-One
> Its Name; he answered: "It is the Wheel of Religion."

[margin note: Altizer's definition of the Incarnation -- the complete self-emptying of God.]

I wept & said: "Is this the law of Jesus,
This terrible devouring sword turning every way?"
He answer'd: "Jesus died because he strove
Against the current of this Wheel; its Name
Is Caiaphas, the dark preacher of Death,
Of sin, of sorrow & of punishment:
Opposing Nature! It is Natural Religion;
But Jesus is the bright Preacher of Life
Creating Nature from this fiery Law
By self-denial & forgiveness of Sin."

We must not imagine that such a condemnation of religion is directed at the non-Christian religious world. It is, rather, Christianity, and Christianity alone, that has reduced human existence to sin and guilt, confronting a broken humanity with a wholly other God who demands a total submission to his numinous and judgmental power. Religion assumes its most repressive form in the Christian religious tradition, because only here—and in its historical antecedent, The Book of Job—may one find a God of naked and absolutely sovereign power, a God who was evolved out of a reversal of the movement of Spirit into flesh, and who now for the first time becomes abstract, alien, lifeless, and alone.

In so far as Christianity continues to speak of God as an Absolute Sovereign it is the enemy of Christ.

The solitary God of the Christian religious tradition certainly embodies a measure of uniqueness: no other religious tradition has so isolated deity and humanity, and all too naturally He finally appears under the forms of Blake's Satan, Hegel's abstract Spirit, and Melville's Moby Dick. Nevertheless, even this most awesome of the forms of God illuminates the unique process of the Christian Word, for it is an evolving Word, a forward-moving Word, a Word that only exists and is real in the concrete life of history. Christianity is a historical faith, not simply because it is grounded in a sacred history of the past, but more deeply because it celebrates the human reality of history as an epiphany of the Word. An incarnate Word embodying a real transfiguration of Spirit into flesh cannot be sought in

God uniquely solitary in Christian tradition

a heavenly beyond, nor can it be reached by a backward movement to primordial time; it is only in the actual and contingent processes of history that Spirit fully becomes flesh. Here, Spirit never truly appears in a pure or eternal form, nor does it simply appear as Spirit, except insofar as it is known apart from its movement into flesh. Moreover, it is only a regressive and religious form of Christianity that would confine the Word to its Biblical and past historical expressions. When the Incarnation is known as a dynamic process of forward movement, then it must be conceived as a progressive movement of Spirit into flesh, even if it should succeed in evoking a religious reversal of its own movement and process. Each historical expression of the Word will bear its own peculiar and distinct reality, and while no clear path may be seen to lie between one and another, faith must ever seek that particular form of the Word which acts in its own present.

Finally, we must conceive the Christian Word as being directed to the eschatological goal of the absolute reversal of flesh and Spirit. Ever since its establishment in the second century, Christian theology has chosen one of two paths: either it has adapted the language of a purely rational and nondialectical thinking, a thinking that wholly isolates theology and faith; or it has become partially dialectical, and thereby attempted to ground its language in the reality of faith only insofar as it has repudiated an eschatological goal. In either case, theology has refused a thinking that would incorporate the apocalyptic ground of the proclamation of Jesus, just as it has turned aside from any attempt to understand the full meaning of an eschatological end. Consequently, Christian theology has never sought to unveil the meaning of an apocalyptic *coincidentia oppositorum*. It is no accident that radical expressions of Christianity have invariably assumed either a dialectical or an apocalyptic form. Apart from a dual and dialectical movement of flesh and Spirit into each other, there can be no actual process of incarnation; here, an original sacred must "descend" and become flesh, just as a fallen flesh must "ascend" and become Spirit. Yet this process cannot be real apart from an actual transfiguration of flesh and Spirit: flesh must cease to exist as flesh in becoming Spirit, even as Spirit must wholly perish as Spirit in fully becoming flesh. The Incarnation can culminate in a truly apocalyptic or eschatological end only by effecting an absolute negation of the original identities of flesh and Spirit. Thereby the given and intrinsic forms of flesh and Spirit are totally reversed so as to make possible a final movement of each into its respective other. Inevitably, the radical Christian believes that the end of the world, whose immediate coming was proclaimed by Jesus, is the total transfiguration of the fallen form of the world, the end of a flesh that is isolated from Spirit, and so likewise the end of a Spirit that is isolated from flesh.

At first glance an apocalyptic *coincidentia oppositorum* would appear to be identical with its mystical counterpart in Oriental religion. Both embody a total dissolution of the "being" of a fallen or profane world, just as each is the fulfillment of a movement of absolute negation, a negation shattering or dissolving an autonomous selfhood, a repressive history, and an exterior cosmos. But does an apocalyptic *coincidentia oppositorum* abolish the opposition between the sacred and the profane by annihilating the reality of flesh or old aeon? True, the religious forms of Christianity have celebrated a Kingdom of God that is wholly Spirit, and lived in hope of the disintegration of the world and the flesh. Even Paul was unable to believe in the resurrection of a fallen flesh, for he posited a wholly negative relationship between flesh and Spirit; and the Gospel of John, which, unlike Paul, abandoned the original apocalyptic ground of Christianity, betrayed its own symbol of the Incarnate Word by envisioning the Kingdom of God in the form of pure Spirit. Let us fully recognize that so to conceive the eschatological destiny of the Word is both to abolish its incarnational form and to renounce the reality

[margin annotations: ? How can flesh cease to exist as flesh apart from death. ?

A. seems to press, ultimately, for a Spirit-flesh unity -- which is basic to ? Neo-Orthodox theology.

A. assumes, I believe incorrectly, that the N.T. undervalues the flesh. Stresses Spirit (N.T.) - according to TJJA] of the Incarnation. Furthermore, we must observe that a religious expression of eschatological faith differs at no decisive point from the purely mystical way of Oriental religion—except for the all too significant fact that eschatological religion has yet to receive a pure expression in history. A truly or radically Christian *coincidentia oppositorum* must pass through an actual transfiguration of flesh and Spirit: each must dialectically move into its own other, as Spirit moves kenotically and historically into flesh, and flesh is transposed into a new and final form of Spirit.

III. FALL AND DEATH

No myth has been more persistent in Christian history, and no religious theme more pervasive, than the myth of the Fall, of man's expulsion from paradise and his consequent condemnation to death. In the perspective of the history of religions, we can sense the significance of this motif by noting that no religion has so stressed the importance and the centrality of the Fall as has Christianity, just as no other religion has accepted the Fall as an ultimate and final event. Almost from its very beginning, moreover, Christianity has paradoxically if partially affirmed that the Fall was a fortunate occurrence, a *felix culpa,* a finally blessed and even necessary event apart from which there could be neither Incarnation nor full redemption. This bitter if liberating knowledge of the loss of paradise is integrally related to the eschatological ground of the Christian faith. Only when the paradise of the Beginning has finally been lost, thereby dissolving the very possibility of a true nostalgia or longing for primordial time, can faith fully give itself to the forward movement of the Christian Word. The Christian may lament the loss of an original paradise, but he himself is banished from its garden.

As we discover the points at which Christianity transcends the universal movement of religion, reversing its in-

[margin handwritten note: No religion has so stressed the myth of the Fall as has Christianity]

trinsic direction and ground, we can only look with amazement upon the obvious fact that throughout its history Christianity has almost invariably appeared in a religious form. Perhaps nothing else could so forcibly demonstrate the theological truth of the historical reality of the Christian Word. Having never appeared in a pure or definitive form, the Christian Word is a Word in process of realizing itself. Inevitably, the Word has only gradually and partially become manifest, appearing in forms that are extrinsic and even antithetical to its own reality, if only as a means of accommodating itself to the actual contingencies of history. Of course, a religious Christianity will dogmatically insist that the Word has been given its definitive and final expression in the Bible. But we must hasten to observe that this is an intrinsically religious claim, exhibiting—insofar as it confines revelation to a past or primordial time—the backward religious movement of return. Nor does such a claim take account of the full and Christian meaning of the Fall. It seeks an unfallen form of the Word, a pure moment of revelation untarnished and unaffected by history, in which the Word is manifest only in its primordial and eternal meaning. Even a Christian belief in the possibility of a final revelation in history is a flight from the truth of the Fall. If Adam has been expelled from paradise, resulting in the advent of a truly profane history, then a final revelation cannot occur in history, apart from a dissolution or reversal of history itself.

In the Orient, where the religious movement of involution, reversal, and return receives its fullest and clearest expression, an absolute or final revelation is always known as occurring in the primordial time of the Beginning. Here, revelation is either wholly isolated from the profane reality of time or is visible in a fallen form only to the extent that it ceases to be absolute and accommodates itself to human ignorance and weakness. When revelation is so conceived, it will be historical only to the extent that it ceases to be revelation. As opposed to this purely religious form of rev-

[margin handwritten notes:] Christianity's emphasis upon the Bible is nothing more or less than an undesirable backward movement.

Has Xity actually ever, in its "ortho-dox forms," said that revelation takes place only in the past events recorded in the Bible? What about personal religious experience? —The internae Testamonium Spiriti Sancti?

elation, a truly historical revelation can only occur in the contingent actuality of a profane history, and thus it must inevitably appear in a fallen rather than an eternal form. Therefore a historical revelation can be manifest in a sacred or eternal form only to the extent that it has not yet become or has ceased to be historical. Revelation can be historical only by means of a metamorphosis of the sacred into the profane, an actual movement of the Word from the sacred to the profane, reversing the backward movement of religion. Religious Christianity resists this movement of the Word, opposing its abandonment of an original and primordial sacred by resurrecting the Word in a religious form. Refusing the Word that appears and is real in the fallen reality of history, the religious Christian succumbs to the temptation of the past by fleeing to the primordial God of an unfallen Beginning.

A fully consistent or radical Christianity knows the totality of the Fall. Consequently, it condemns the religious quest for an unfallen sacred, repudiates the God who alone is God, and renounces all attachment to the past. Blake's prophetic hatred of memory, his realization that "Innocence" must become "Experience," and his subsequent attack upon innocence as a subhuman flight from the human reality of history all illustrate this antireligious ground of radical Christianity. Having been initiated into the totally fallen and historical reality of the world, the radical Christian knows that the original paradise is both lost and forbidden, lost in the sense that it has wholly vanished from history, and forbidden if only because a quest for an original paradise must reverse the reality of history, a reversal that can be accomplished only by abolishing humanity. To speak of the totality of the Fall is to recognize that no way lies present in history to an unfallen innocence or a primordial Word. Once history has become truly manifest in its fully profane form, both an original paradise and a primordial sacred have been forever lost. Confronted with the advent of a totally profane world, faith has an inevitable temptation to flee to the past. Yet radical Christianity points the way to a new epiphany of the Word—a Word that has died in its original and sacred form, and is now manifest only at the center of the radical profane.

If we are to grant that the Christian Word is truly a forward-moving process, and moves by way of a metamorphosis of the sacred into the profane, then it can move only by negating its original identity, thereby passing through the death of its original form. Christianity has always celebrated death as the way to redemption, proclaiming that Christ's death inaugurated a new reality of joy and forgiveness, and calling all men to a participation in his death as the way of salvation. Death, it is true, is a universal motif in the history of religions: man dies to his profane or fallen condition as a means of being reborn in the sacred. However, Christianity, and Christianity alone, proclaims the death of the sacred; and only in Christianity do we find a concrete experience of the factuality and the finality of death. At this point Buddhism presents an instructive contrast to Christianity, for here one discovers unbelievably complex systems of meditation centering upon the image of death, but here death is a way to the dissolution of the human condition, and therefore to the abolition of pain and suffering. No other higher religion in the world calls its participants to a full experience of the pain and darkness of the human act of dying as the way to transfiguration and rebirth. Unique, too, is the way in which the Christian is called to share or to coexperience Christ's death, where a sharing of the passion of Christ becomes a participation in the process of salvation. Underlying this Christian experience of death is a new openness to death as an ultimately real event. Nowhere else is death granted its simple if brutal reality, for nowhere else in history has man found life through the human event of death.

Once again, however, we must note that the historical forms of Christianity have thus far failed to embody the full

[margin note:] The process of secularization must continue until the divine commits suicide by totally emptying itself into the secular.

and radical consequences of the Christian Word. Not only did unchristian ideas of immortality creep into the body of Christianity, but the very religious form of traditional Christianity has foreclosed the possibility of its acceptance of the finality of death. A belief in the resurrection of Jesus in the form of an eternal and primordial God must necessarily annul the reality of his death, either reducing it to a mere transition to a higher state or retrogressively conceiving it as an abolition of his human condition. Unlike the doctrinal expressions of orthodox Christianity, Christian meditation upon the passion of Christ has grasped his death as an ultimate and human event, a concrete but decisive event that has transformed the primordial relation between man and God. Despite its claim of being a historical faith, orthodox Christianity tenaciously clings to the primordial Creator, an eternal and unchanging Lord. Thus it is closed to the presence in Christ's passion of God himself. Trinitarian forms of Christianity have inevitably dissolved the actual and the historical reality of the Crucifixion and the Incarnation, because in identifying Christ with an eternal Word they have eliminated the possibility of either actual death or real movement. Therewith, too, they have retreated from the factuality and finality of death, for death cannot be real in the presence of an eternal and primordial Word.

Only when the Fall is known as a real and decisive event does death assume its awesome reality. A religion that is innocent of the damning knowledge of the finality of the Fall cannot know the true reality of death, for insofar as an eternal and impassive Word is present to the religious consciousness death can pose no ultimate threat to the believer. Before death can become fully actualized and wholly real to consciousness it must penetrate the realm of the sacred, appearing here not simply as an image of the profane but, rather, affecting by the fullness of its own actuality the very form and reality of the sacred. Christian imagery of death, perhaps most so in the New Testament, has ever tended to regress to a pre-Christian religious form, dissolving the reality of death in its vision of resurrection, thereby confining death to temporal contingency and fallen flesh. Such a reversal of the full meaning of death inevitably resists the finality of the Fall, isolating Word and Fall by clinging to an unfallen and imperishable Word, and annulling the historical actuality of the Fall by positing its culmination in a prefallen Spirit. Moreover, when the finality of the Fall has been so reversed, the Incarnation and the Crucifixion can no longer be manifest as fully historical events, because here the Word can only be present in a prefallen and hence nonhistorical form. No true movement is possible for a Word that is unaffected by its own action and process; accordingly, the real ground of religious Christianity is an impassive and unmoving Word.

Again and again we have discovered that Christianity has resisted the Word of its own proclamation by regressing to a primordial, an unfallen, and a nonhistorical Word. Above all, it is faith's resistance to the Word's becoming fully actualized as flesh that has driven it to the backward movement of religion. Rather than opening itself to the forward movement of the Word, with its intrinsic goal of undergoing a total metamorphosis in history, Christianity has given itself to a dualistic isolation of flesh from Spirit, thereby imprisoning the Word in an inactive and lifeless form. Not until the Word has been liberated from its religious veil will it appear and be real to the Christian in its own intrinsic reality. Yet this can occur only when the Word is known as undergoing an actual movement into history, wherein the Word itself is affected by its movement, abandoning its original and primordial form as it becomes incarnate, and moving forward to the goal of a new and eschatological Totality. An incarnate Word that ✳ truly and actually enters the profane reality of history must not only appear in a fallen form, but must itself pass through the reality of Fall and death, thereby emptying itself of its original purity and power. The Christian Word itself is a fallen or kenotically emptied Word, just as the Incarnation is the truest witness to the totality and finality of the Fall. Now the Word is active and real *only* in the profane reality of a fallen history. In the Crucifixion the Word has finally died to its original form, losing its transcendent glory and its primordial holiness, while fully becoming flesh. Only in the Crucifixion, in the death of the Word on the Cross, does the Word actually and wholly become flesh. Finally, the Incarnation is only truly and actually real if it effects the death of the original sacred, the death of God himself.

II

Jesus and the Incarnation

I. THE NAME OF JESUS

WHY JESUS? Christianity has always been confronted from
both within and from without by the primary question of
why it makes such an absolute claim for the particular
person of Jesus. At no time has this question become so
compelling as it has today, as Christianity is attempting
to move beyond its past historical expression to a universal
form, and is inevitably being forced to face the full scandal
of its own particularity. What is the intrinsic relationship
between the Christian faith and Jesus of Nazareth? Can
and should the Christian Word be divorced from the person of Jesus? What can the name of Jesus mean to the
Christian today or, for that matter, to any man living outside of Christendom? Is his name nameable in our time?
Is Jesus present in our history? Before we can meet these
questions, we must first inquire of the identity of Jesus,
recognizing that modern New Testament scholarship has
for the most part dissolved the image of Jesus in the
Christian tradition, and acknowledging, if only on the
basis of the Gospel accounts of his teaching, that Jesus
will be present to later ages in strange and paradoxical
forms.

In the radical Christian vision, as can most clearly be
seen in Blake, Hegel, and Nietzsche, we invariably find
the prophetic judgment that the Jesus of the Christian tradition is alien and lifeless, having been born only by means
of a negation of the original Jesus, and therewith having

evolved to the very opposite of his original identity. Moreover, the radical Christian insists that Jesus can never again
be manifest as the man whom his disciples knew, that
Jesus died on the cross; and while an image of the dead
Jesus has been perpetuated by Christian orthodoxy, albeit
in the mask of the God-man or the eternal Word, the true
Jesus has passed through his death from a particular to a
universal form, and continues to be present in a forward-
moving and transfiguring Word. Nevertheless, even the
radical Christian either clings to the name of Jesus or preserves it in a disguised form. Just as Nietzsche reverenced
Jesus, hailing him as a free spirit who had abolished religion and consequently made possible a new man who is
free of guilt and its corresponding resentment, so likewise
Hegel came to know Jesus as the kenotic Word or "pure
negativity" that is the source of all life and movement, and
Blake called upon all mankind to accept the goal of becoming identical with Jesus—he gave the motto, "Jesus
only," to his greatest work, *Jerusalem*—proclaiming that
Jesus is the "Universal Humanity." The name of Jesus is
no mere symbol of a higher man to these prophets: rather,
they unveil the historical reality and power of his name as
concealing a hidden but universal process of redemption
and transformation, a process that has only been known in
a reversed or religious form to his ecclesiastical followers.
No way lies to the living Jesus, proclaim these radical
Christian prophets, apart from a total transcendence of the
orthodox Christian tradition.

Setting aside for the moment the problem of Christianity's betrayal of Jesus, can we discover in the Christian affirmation of the name of Jesus a clearly distinct and
individual movement of faith? What distinguishes the
Christian proclamation of Jesus from the devotional or
bhakti forms of Hinduism and Buddhism? First, we cannot fail to note that Christianity limits the name of the redeemer to the historical name of Jesus, whereas bhakti religion can either be open to a wide variety of savior gods

and goddesses as in Hinduism, or it can follow the Buddhist way of devotion to a single savior deity (Amitabha or Amida) who is wholly dissociated from the historical founder of the religion (Siddhartha Gautama). By this means we can see that the scandal of Christianity's particularity is inseparably related to the historical ground of its faith; and a faith arising in response to a unique and particular event can only lose the name or reality of that event by ceasing to be itself. But where lies the uniqueness of the original event or person of Jesus? Historically or phenomenologically considered, that uniqueness must in some sense lie in the fact that here and only here a sacred event deeply and decisively affects the concrete process of history, embedding itself in a particular and contingent movement in such a way as to be indissolubly identified with the actuality of its occurrence, thereby abandoning the universal or eternal form that otherwise is invariably present in sacred events. When the Christian pronounces the name of Jesus, he is confessing his participation in the actuality lying at the center of this unique and particular event. The "Experience" that Blake envisioned as the dialectical contrary of "Innocence," the full actuality (*Wirklichkeit*) that Hegel knew to be the destiny of Spirit, the Yes-saying to life, the body, and the earth that Nietzsche opposed to all No-saying, are all expressions of this uniquely Christian movement of faith. What is new in the Christian name of Jesus is the epiphany of the totality of the sacred in the contingency of a particular moment of time: in this name the sacred appears and is real only to the extent that it becomes actual and realized in history.

Therefore we cannot truly pronounce the name of Jesus if we isolate his name from the contingency and the actuality of our concrete existence in the world. It was the religious movement away from this immediate actuality that constituted an important dimension of Christianity's betrayal of Jesus, for when Jesus appears as an eternal and cosmic Word, he loses the immediacy of his original ap-

pearance. Yet it is no less true that to identify Jesus
wholly with a particular and isolated person or event of
the past is to foreclose the possibility of his present life or
forward movement. Indeed, we can know Jesus as the
ancient Jesus of Nazareth only insofar as we are closed to
his contemporary presence. Not only is this ancient Jesus
alien and lifeless, but precisely for this reason he can be
manifest in a religious form only as an abstract and distant
Word or as an epiphany of a primordial Innocence. In
either case we find a reversal of concrete experience, a
flight from the actuality of consciousness and the body, a
regression to a primordial moment of time. The uniquely
Christian Jesus is the Jesus who is fully manifest in a
present and actual moment of time. Accordingly, Blake
could speak of his prophetic call in these words:

> This theme calls me in sleep night after night,
>   & ev'ry morn
> Awakes me at sun-rise; then I see the Saviour over
>   me
> Spreading his beams of love & dictating the words
>   of this mild song.
>
> "Awake! awake O sleeper of the land of shadows,
>   wake! expand!
> I am in you and you in me, mutual in love divine:
> Fibres of love from man to man thro' Albion's
>   pleasant land.
> . . . .
> I am not a God afar off, I am a brother and
>   friend:
> Within your bosoms I reside, and you reside in
>   me."
>
>   (*Jerusalem* 4:3-20.)

Now, it is not simply any moment of time that is fully
actual and real, for the mere passage of time is not to be
identified as actuality, just as the brute factuality of history
cannot reveal a human hand or face. Only a fully lived time

is actual and immediate, its actuality deriving from a fullness of life that its movement releases, as time here receives a fully human expression. One of the most profound
portraits of such actuality, and one that we must regard as
embodying a vision of the Jesus who is present in our time,
is contained in Nietzsche's *Thus Spoke Zarathustra,* a
work that was intended to be an ironic reversal of the
Christian gospel. In the section entitled "On Redemption,"
in the second part, Zarathustra reveals that the presence
of time in a past and external form is the deepest obstacle
to the realization of life and joy:

> "To redeem those who lived in the past and to recreate
> all 'it was' into a 'thus I willed it'—that alone should I
> call redemption. Will—that is the name of the liberator
> and joy-bringer; thus I taught you, my friends. But now
> learn this too: the will itself is still a prisoner. Willing
> liberates; but what is it that puts even the liberator him-
> self in fetters? 'It was'—that is the name of the will's
> gnashing of teeth and most secret melancholy. Powerless
> against what has been done, he is an angry spectator of
> all that is past. The will cannot will backwards; and that
> he cannot break time and time's covetousness, that is the
> will's loneliest melancholy."

A spirit of revenge is born of this melancholy, what Nietzsche calls the will's ill will against time and its "it was," a
religious rebellion against the mere fact of time, leading to
the refusal of time itself, and a consequent orgy of self-
hatred as a broken humanity seeks to dissolve itself by
ceasing to will. Yet Zarathustra, in announcing a new redemption, speaks to the very madness of the vengeful No-
sayer:

> "I led you away from these fables when I taught you,
> 'The will is a creator.' All 'it was' is a fragment, a riddle,
> a dreadful accident—until the creative will says to it,
> 'But thus I willed it.' Until the creative will says to it,
> 'But thus I will it; thus shall I will it.' "

On its surface there seems to be no relationship between this passage and a Christian witness to the immediate presence of Jesus, for the "creative will" is equated by Zarathustra with the will to power, and is judged to be its own redeemer and joy-bringer. Nevertheless, Zarathustra's goal is to "will backwards," to transform the dreadful accident of all "it was" into "thus I will it" or "thus shall I will it," thereby making possible a Yes-saying to the oppressive contingency of time. Yes-saying is a reversal of the No-saying of the spirit of revenge or *ressentiment;* it freely accepts and affirms the burden of time, but its affirmation transforms the external givenness of time into the human actuality of a time that is fully lived and immediate. Yet in what sense may we speak here of the Jesus who is near and not afar off? Why in any way associate Zarathustra with Jesus? We do so first because Nietzsche himself opposed Zarathustra to Christianity, but more deeply because his portrait of Jesus in *The Antichrist* bears an amazing resemblance to Zarathustra, since the original Jesus, like the new Zarathustra, is here conceived to be the opposite of the Christian Christ:

> Make no mistake at this point, however seductive the Christian, in other words, the *ecclesiastical,* prejudice may be: such a symbolist par excellence stands outside all religion, all cult concepts, all history, all natural science, all experience of the world, all knowledge, all politics, all psychology, all books, all art—his "knowledge" is *pure foolishness* precisely concerning the fact that such things exist. *Culture* is not known to him even by hearsay, he does not need to fight it—he does not negate it. The same applies to the state, to the whole civic order and society, to work, to war—he never had any reason to negate "the world"; the ecclesiastical concept of "world" never occurred to him. To negate is the very thing that is impossible for him. (Section 32.)

The Jesus who is incapable of negating the world is for that very reason free of all *ressentiment:* he cannot even know a world standing over against the blessedness that he proclaims to be the only reality.

> In the whole psychology of the "evangel" the concept of guilt and punishment is lacking; also the concept of reward. "Sin"—any distance separating God and man—is abolished: *precisely this is the "glad tidings."* Blessedness is not promised, it is not tied to conditions: it is the only reality—the rest is a sign with which to speak of it. (Section 33.)

Nietzsche even goes so far as to say that the life and death of Jesus was nothing other than the practice of blessedness. Therefore, Jesus could know nothing of the dreadful accident of "it was"; his practice of blessedness must inevitably have transformed all "it was" into a "thus I willed it"—although words such as "I" and "will" here lose their common meaning and consequently Nietzsche freely acknowledged that Jesus was the original liberator from the No-saying of guilt and revenge.

Whether or not we can accept Zarathustra as a radical Christian image of Jesus—and this is an interpretation that will only gradually be explored in the course of this book—it should be clear that a redemption from a past and external time, which paradoxically occurs by way of affirmation rather than negation, cannot be dissociated from a reversal of the religious movement of involution and return. If the original Jesus abolished or reversed religion, thereby annulling the quest for the primordial Beginning, then he himself can never appear in a moment of lost time, nor can he be truly present in any form of Innocence. A "Christian" quest for lost time must invert the Jesus who dissolved the religious movement of remembrance and return. But by opening ourselves to the immediate actuality of the moment before us, we can know the Jesus who is present in the fullness of time itself, even if that time should prove to be a negation or reversal of the past event of Jesus of Nazareth.

II. KENOSIS

If the Christian name of Jesus is in some intimate and unique sense associated with the immediate actuality of the present, then the God of the Christian tradition is not simply a primordial deity but, rather, the God who has evolved out of a religious reversal of the act of Incarnation. The "atheism" of the radical Christian is in large measure a prophetic reaction to a distant and nonredemptive God who by virtue of his very sovereignty and transcendence stands wholly apart from the forward movement and the historical presence of the Incarnate Word. It is precisely because the radical Christian seeks a total union with the Word made flesh that he must refuse the God who alone is God and give himself to a quest for the God who *is* Jesus. When Christian Scholasticism followed Aristotle in defining God as pure actuality or *actus purus,* it wholly isolated God from the world, knowing him as inactive and impassive, the God who is aseitic, or self-derived, the *causa sui* who is the sole cause of himself. At the very time when this Scholastic definition was being baptized by the Church, a contrary vision of God arose in Christian mysticism, a vision arising from an experience of God in the depths of the human soul where God is known as generating the individual soul as the eternal Son of God. The radical Christian mystic knew that he himself was generated as the Son of God, the same Son, and without distinction. Meister Eckhart coined a word to express this idea, *istigkeit,* with various spellings, meaning "isness" in an immediate sense; thus he declared in his own official defense: "God's isness is my isness, and neither more nor less." Eckhart could even affirm in one of his sermons that God is that One who denies of every other that it is anything except himself. While this radical expression of Christian mysticism was driven underground by the ecclesiastical authorities of the Church, it continued to exist in a subterranean form, finally surfacing in Jakob Böhme

and his circle, who provided the germinal source for the
one thinker who created a conceptual portrait of the incarnate or kenotic movement of God: Hegel.

We cannot hope within the brief compass of this study to
set forth the full meaning of Hegel's idea of absolute or
pure negativity, but it is the center of his dialectical system, and it cannot finally be divorced from a Christian
ground. Negativity is the power and the process of the
self-realization or the self-mediation of the Hegelian Absolute, Subject or Spirit. Accordingly, Spirit is the kenotic
or emptying process of negativity; as such it is the true
actuality (*Wirklichkeit*) of the world, for Spirit is the in-
herently negative or the negativity found in Being *per se*.
As Hegel says in the section on revealed religion in *The
Phenomenology of Spirit,* Spirit qua essential Being is
"absolute distinction from itself, is pure process of becoming its other." Hegel's dialectical method succeeds in
effecting an inversion of the Western ontological tradition,
for he does not simply negate the root idea of the aseity
of Being, he reverses this idea by conceiving Being as a
perpetual process of becoming its own other, a process
that is known in myth or religious belief as the self-sacrifice of the divine Being. Despite the fact that Hegel has
been damned by theologians for transposing faith into
philosophical thinking, it is only in Hegel that we may discover an idea of God or Being or Spirit which embodies
an understanding of the theological meaning of the Incarnation. No doubt Hegel's abstract language disguises
the Christian faith that is its source, but rather than falling
back upon a pre-Christian and even primordial understanding of Being, Hegel opened the very center of his thinking
to the Incarnate Word of faith, allowing its kenotic movement to be the archetype of what he conceived as the dialectical method of pure thinking. True, the traditional deposit of Christian dogma is transformed in Hegel, and now
it appears as no more than the portal to true understanding. But this is exactly the case with all radical Christians,

who invariably believe that the final age of the Spirit effects
a negation and transcendence of the dogma of the Church.

The kenotic meaning of Spirit is already given in the
preface to *The Phenomenology of Spirit,* a meaning that
Hegel says is due to the modern age and its religion. Yet
Hegel transforms the mythological language of Christianity by understanding the emptying of Spirit to be the self-
expression of Spirit in an objective and seemingly alien
form:

> Spirit is alone Reality. It is the inner being of the world,
> that which essentially is, and is *per se;* it assumes objec-
> tive, determinate form, and enters into relations with it-
> self—it is externality (otherness), and exists for-self; yet,
> in this determination, and in its otherness, it is still one with
> itself—it is self-contained and self-complete, in-itself and
> for-itself at once.

However, these words must not be misconstrued as speaking of a traditional monistic pantheism. Whereas a mystical or ontological monism conceives Spirit as the underlying and ultimate identity of a world that is only
apparently or provisionally external and temporal, Hegel,
and Hegel alone, reached a radically dialectical understanding of Spirit wherein only Spirit is ultimately real, and
yet Spirit is fully identical with itself when it exists as the
world or as an external "otherness." To employ Hegel's
terminology, Spirit exists "for-itself" (*für sich*) when it
exists as its own opposite or other; nevertheless, this
seemingly fallen or lower existence of Spirit is both self-
contained and self-complete, or for-itself and in-itself (*an
sich*) at once. Only the modern age and its religion unveils the actual identity of Spirit with its own other. For
while Spirit is implicitly a self-contained Totality, it is
only in the modern world that Spirit reaches its absolute
form by becoming actually and historically self-conscious
of itself.

Historians of philosophy tell us that the one truly unique

ground of Hegel's thinking is his dialectical understanding of pure or radical negation, a self-negation of Spirit in which Spirit kenotically becomes its own other, existing as the actual opposite of its own original or initial identity. This self-negation of Spirit makes possible its real movement, a historical movement in which Spirit evolves to its absolute form only by progressively negating its own expressions. Thus Spirit, which exists originally and eternally in-itself (*an sich*), must become historical, existing in a determinate form as object for-itself (*für sich*).

> It has to become self-contained for itself (*für sich*), on its own account; it must be knowledge of Spirit, and must be consciousness of itself as Spirit. This means, it must be presented to itself as an object, but at the same time straightway annul and transcend this objective form; it must be its own object in which it finds itself reflected.

Only when Spirit knows itself in its own otherness will it fulfill its destiny as Spirit, for unlike all forms of dialectical religious understanding, Hegel conceives of Spirit as a forward movement of self-negation or "self-redemption." This forward movement of Spirit is made possible only by an actual process of self-negation: Spirit-in-itself negates itself and thus becomes Spirit-for-itself; and by the negation of negation Spirit-for-itself transcends itself and once more becomes Spirit-in-itself; yet this final form of Spirit is far richer and fuller than its initial beginning.

Such an abstract and abbreviated exposition, of course, does very little to make clear Hegel's understanding of Spirit. Significantly enough, this understanding appears most clearly in *The Phenomenology of Spirit* when Hegel employs the actual language of *kenōsis*. Hegel can speak, for example, of the "*kenōsis* of the eternal Being," whereby it enters the sphere of actuality, becoming sensuous and uncomprehended. While existing in its kenotic form, Spirit can never be apprehended as pure Spirit, and must instead be known as the opposite or otherness of Spirit. Quite naturally Hegel believes that religion knows only the extrinsic form of Spirit, it apprehends Spirit through imaginative representation or *Vorstellung,* a representation expressing merely the external form of Spirit, a form in which Spirit appears to transcend the actuality of history and consciousness. Yet a dialectical understanding of the phenomenon of religion can lead to a true conception of the kenotic process of pure negativity. For example, Hegel's analysis of the cultic act of sacrifice shows that this very act points to the original and implicit self-sacrifice of Spirit.

> The self actively sacrificing demonstrates in actual existence, and sets before its own consciousness, this already implicitly completed self-renunciation on the part of absolute Being; and replaces that immediate reality, which absolute Being has, by the higher, viz. that of the self making the sacrifice.

Paradoxically, the implicitly completed self-sacrifice of Spirit only becomes realized or historically actualized in self-consciousness while Spirit is in a state of alienation and estrangement from itself. This self-sacrifice enters consciousness when Spirit first appears in its kenotic form as the man, Jesus of Nazareth. The primitive Christian community marks the historical or actual advent of Absolute Spirit because for the first time consciousness recognizes God in immediate present existence, and God is known as self-consciousness because he is beheld sensuously and immediately as the individual self of Jesus.

> This incarnation of the Divine Being, its having essentially and directly the shape of self-consciousness, is the simple content of Absolute Religion. Here the Divine Being is known as Spirit; this religion is the Divine Being's consciousness concerning itself that it is Spirit. For Spirit is knowledge of self in a state of alienation of self: Spirit is the Being which is the process of retaining identity with itself in its otherness.

The last sentence is one of Hegel's clearest definitions of Spirit, and not only does it unveil the kenotic form of Spirit, it expresses the conceptual meaning of the God who has died in Jesus, the God who has negated himself in fully and finally becoming flesh.

Already in the Gospel of John we find the revolutionary Christian proclamation that God *is* love. But despite the fact that Christian faith has invariably given witness to the reality of the compassion of God, Christian theology has been unable to incorporate this primary core of faith if only because it has ever remained bound to an idea of God as a wholly self-sufficient, self-enclosed, and absolutely autonomous Being. Even when theologians have rediscovered the *agapē* or total self-giving of God, they have confined it to the movement of the Incarnation, and thus have dualistically isolated God's love from the primordial nature and existence of God himself. So long as God is known in his primordial form as an eternal and unchanging Being, he can never be known in his incarnate form as self-giving or self-negating Being. The radical Christian refuses to speak of God's existence—Hegel appropriately speaks in his *Logic* of the soulless word "is"—because he knows that God has negated and transcended himself in the Incarnation, and thereby he has fully and finally ceased to exist in his original or primordial form. To know that God *is* Jesus, is to know that God himself has become flesh: no longer does God exist as transcendent Spirit or sovereign Lord, now God *is* love.

If nothing else, the contemporary Christian can be initiated by Hegel into an understanding of a dialectical movement of God or Being or Spirit, an actual movement or process reflecting and incorporating the kenotic reality of the Incarnate Word. In *The Phenomenology of Spirit,* there are three fundamental moments of Spirit: (1) essential Being, in which Spirit is simultaneously in- and for-itself; (2) explicit Self-existence, which is the express "otherness" of essential Being, and for which that Being is "object"; and (3) Self-existence or Self-knowledge *in* that other. Appropriately, Hegel speaks most explicitly about these moments in the section on revealed religion, and then he goes on to say that in its third moment Spirit apprehends itself *only* in the objective otherness of its Self-existence:

> In this emptying itself, in this *kenōsis,* it is merely within itself: the independent Self-existence which excludes itself from essential Being is the knowledge of itself on the part of essential Being. It is the "Word," the *Logos,* which when spoken empties the speaker of himself, outwardizes him, and leaves him behind emptied, but the Word is as immediately perceived, and only this act of self-perceiving himself is the actual existence of the "Word."

We must not be misled by these words into thinking that Hegel in speaking of the self-knowledge of Spirit is referring to any kind of scientific, objective, or merely rational knowledge. Rather, he is speaking of a final or even apocalyptic knowledge, a knowledge that only dawns in the third age or moment of Spirit, and a knowledge presupposing an absolute self-negation of Spirit's original moment or mode. Cryptic as his language is when Hegel speaks most dialectically, can the Christian doubt that the "Word" which when spoken empties the speaker of himself is the Incarnate Word? God himself is left behind and "emptied" by the movement of the Incarnation and now the Word *is* only as it is immediately perceived in the act of "self-perceiving himself." An immediate perception in this sense is dialectical; the self perceives itself only in its intrinsic otherness: only by an actual but total reversal of its original moment or mode can Spirit know and fulfill itself as independent "Self-existence."

God *is* Jesus, proclaims the radical Christian, and by this he means that the Incarnation is a total and all-consuming act: as Spirit becomes the Word that empties the Speaker of himself, the whole reality of Spirit becomes incarnate in its opposite. Only the radical Christian witnesses to the full reality of Jesus or the Incarnate Word, because he alone responds to the totally kenotic movement of God. If Spirit truly empties itself in entering the world, then its own essential or original Being must be left behind in an empty and lifeless form. Now, Spirit can exist and be real only in a kenotic or incarnate mode that is the very opposite of its original Being. Hegel and the radical Christian would teach us that finally Spirit is this eternal movement of absolute self-negation. Apart from what Hegel called the process of absolute negativity, there lies no way of apprehending the ontological reality of the Incarnation, and unless the Incarnation is known as effecting an absolute negation of the primordial or essential Being of God, there can be no knowledge that God *is* love. A Christian proclamation of the love of God is a proclamation that God has negated himself in becoming flesh, his Word is now the opposite or the intrinsic otherness of his primordial Being, and God himself has ceased to exist in his original mode as transcendent or disincarnate Spirit: God *is* Jesus.

III. THE UNIVERSAL HUMANITY

When Blake named Jesus as the "Universal Humanity" he was speaking of the Incarnate Word who is both the source and the substance of all life, and this very comprehensiveness of Blake's vision of Jesus demanded not only that he sacrifice the historical and imaginative particularity of the Church's Christ but also impelled him to seek the presence of Jesus in that world of experience most estranged from the Christ of Christian orthodoxy. Nothing less than a kenotic vision of Jesus underlies Blake's mature prophetic work, and by coming to see that Blake and Hegel share a common vision of Christ we can grasp the fundamental unity of radical Christianity. As early as the *Songs of Innocence,* Jesus appears in Blake's poetry under the figures of the lamb and the shepherd and in the universal human virtues of mercy, pity, peace, and love ("The Divine Image"). But here his most passionate presence is in "On Another's Sorrow," which opens with the famous lines:

> Can I see another's woe,
> And not be in sorrow too?
> Can I see another's grief,
> And not seek for kind relief?

However, the "I" of this lyric is Jesus himself, who is identified in the penultimate stanza as the maker of all those who suffer and lament; and then the poem reaches this conclusion:

> O! he gives to us his joy
> That our grief he may destroy;
> Till our grief is fled & gone
> He doth sit by us and moan.

At about the same time or shortly before he wrote this lyric, Blake concluded the aphorisms which comprise *There Is No Natural Religion* with an affirmation of the Incarnation: "Therefore God becomes as we are, that we may be as he is." While these words parallel one of the Church's earliest theological formulations of the meaning of the Incarnation, Blake gives them a contrary meaning. For he is not speaking of a transcendent and wholly other Godhead but rather of the God who has fully and finally become flesh. It was the simple humanity of Jesus that attracted Blake's devotion, he saw that humanity wherever there is pain or joy; and while condemning all notions of an abstract or general humanity, he profoundly believed that Jesus is the body of humanity, and is present in every human hand and face:

> The Divine Vision still was seen,
> Still was the Human Form Divine,
> Weeping in weak & mortal clay,
> O Jesus, still the Form was thine.
> (*Jerusalem* 27:57-60.)

A fundamental problem posed by the radical Christian vision of Christ is the concrete identity of the Incarnate Word. Here, as we have seen, the Word is not confined to the particular man, Jesus of Nazareth; nor is it to be identified with the exalted Christ who is present in the images and the cultus of the Church; nor, for that matter, can the kenotic Word be equated with the Lamb of Innocence. No, the totally incarnate Word can only be the Jesus who is present in what Blake called "Experience," the Jesus who is actually and fully incarnate in every human hand and face. The radical Christian knows that God has truly died in Jesus and that his death has liberated humanity from the oppressive presence of the primordial Being. Indeed, Blake's most exalted vision would teach us that humanity can only exist through this death of God in Jesus:

> Jesus said: "Wouldest thou love one who never died
> For thee, or ever die for one who had not died for thee?
> And if God dieth not for Man & giveth not himself
> Eternally for Man, Man could not exist; for Man is Love
> As God is Love: every kindness to another is a little Death
> In the Divine Image, nor can Man exist but by Brotherhood."
>
> (*Jerusalem* 96:23-28.)

If, as Blake declares, the "Divine Mercy" redeems man in the "Body of Jesus" (*Jerusalem* 36:54), it does so only by freely dying in Jesus; and that death is both a once-and-for-all event annihilating God as the Wholly Other, and a death that is repeated in God's eternal death for "Man." A death that is consummated in such an eternal repetition is obviously not confined to the particular death of Jesus, nor can an eternal repetition of the divine death be enclosed within the faith and liturgy of the Church: to

the extent that the death of God in Jesus is limited to a
particular time and space, the full reality and comprehensiveness of that death is negated, and God dies only to be
resurrected in his original and primordial form.

What is that humanity which can only exist as a consequence of God's dying for man? Obviously Blake is not
speaking of what he himself condemned as the natural
man, as can be seen from his address, "To The Deists," in
Jerusalem: "Man is born a Spectre or Satan & is altogether
an Evil, & requires a New Selfhood continually, & must
continually be changed into his direct Contrary." A new
humanity is created by the death of God in Jesus, a humanity that is a direct contrary of the natural man who is
isolated in his own selfhood and imprisoned by the brute
contingency of time. As early as *The Marriage of Heaven
and Hell,* while answering the question, "Is not God alone
the Prolific?" Blake answers: "God only Acts & Is, in existing beings or Men." The Jesus who is the "Universal Humanity" is the full coming together of God and man: the
God who has given himself eternally for man has thereby
ceased to exist as a self-enclosed and autonomous Being,
and the new man who is born in Jesus is liberated by the
death of God from the oppressive power of every alien
reality standing over against and beyond humanity. With
the death of God, a primordial Being existing in-itself as
its own creation or ground has been shattered, and with its
dissolution every alien other loses its intrinsic ground. Now
a new humanity arises that can give itself to the immediate
actuality of the present as a result of being liberated from
the once-and-for-all givenness of a primordial and distant
Being. Blake calls this new humanity the "Body of Jesus,"
not because it is the crucified body in the tomb, or the
Lord of the Resurrection and the Ascension but, rather,
because it is the incarnate body of the God who has
eternally died for man, and hence it could be hailed by
Blake as "The Eternal Great Humanity Divine."

Once again we see the theological implications of a

radical Christian affirmation of the Incarnation: in dying
to his primordial and transcendent form, God himself becomes fully incarnate in the "Word" or "Body" of Jesus,
and thus he ceases to be present or real as the God who
alone is God. Or we could also express this truth of radical
faith in Blakean terms by saying that the death of God in
Jesus effects a transition from Innocence to Experience:
humanity is banished from the original paradise of Eden—
which Blake calls "Beulah"—the timelessness of that paradise is now at best a momentary release from the burden
of time, for Innocence is forbidden the Christian who has
been initiated by Jesus into the actuality of Experience. We
might even say that Jesus is the Christian name of the totality of Experience, a new actuality created by the abolition
of the primordial Being, whose death inaugurates a new
humanity liberated from all transcendent norms and meaning. But with this new actuality there also comes a terrible
darkness resulting from the obliteration of all inherited
and established forms of judgment and understanding. So
revolutionary was this actuality that it was not until after
eighteen centuries that it penetrated the historical body of
Christendom, first appearing in an anti-Christian form,
and then finally eroding the foundations of the whole
Western historical tradition. Yet the very darkness brought
on by the historical actualization of the death of God
makes possible the movement of the Incarnate Word into
the universal body of humanity:

> And thine the Human Face, & thine
> The Human Hands & Feet & Breath,
> Entering thro' the Gates of Birth
> And passing thro' the Gates of Death.
> (*Jerusalem* 27:61-64.)

Jesus cannot appear as the "Universal Humanity" until
the transcendent realm has been emptied and darkened;
with the eclipse of that realm no primordial archetype or
paradigm remains present in consciousness, since humanity

evolves to a fully universal and historical form only with the disappearance of its ground in a Being that is confined to a primordial or particular moment of time. We must recall that the modern historical consciousness is little more than two hundred years old, and that it was born by means of an eclipse of the transcendent realm, an eclipse resulting in the birth of a unique sense of historical particularity, a historicity arising from the advent of a fully actualized process of concrete and historical time. For the first time historical events appeared as radically particular, as confined in their meaning and value to the actual but singular process in which they occur, and thus as being wholly detached from a universal order or law. Despite the fact that modern Christian theologians have long lauded Christianity as a historical faith, they have for the most part conceived of salvation history in priestly terms as an isolated but absolute and once-and-for-all series of events of the past; or, insofar as they have identified the moment of salvation or "decision" with a contemporary historicity, they have conceived of historicity as a purely inward or subjective realm, existing totally apart from the actuality and the contingency of the concrete processes of history. If only in reaction against the "anti-Christian" Hegel, few if any theologians have been able to accept and affirm the actual process of history as salvation history. Indeed, the theologian must inevitably remain closed to the redemptive possibilities of our history unless he is prepared to affirm the death of God as an epiphany of Christ.

True, our history has progressively but decisively dissolved every sign and image of the Christ who was once present in the Church. Yet the name of Jesus can continue to embody the innermost reality of faith if it can make concretely present the total union of God and man, even if that union should finally obliterate the God of a former faith. As the God who *is* Jesus becomes ever more deeply incarnate in the body of humanity, he loses every semblance of his former visage, until he appears wherever there is energy and life. Blake's Los or the "Human Imagination" can employ a traditional mystical language to speak of the apocalyptic Eden in which this God will be all in all:

> "Mutual in one another's love and wrath all renewing
> We live as One Man; for contracting our infinite senses
> We behold multitude, or expanding, we behold as one,
> As One Man all the Universal Family, and that One Man
> We call Jesus the Christ; and he in us, and we in him
> Live in perfect harmony in Eden, the land of life,
> Giving, receiving, and forgiving each other's trespasses.
> He is the Good shepherd, he is the Lord and master,
> He is the Shepherd of Albion, he is all in all,
> In Eden, in the garden of God, and in heavenly Jerusalem."
>
> (*Jerusalem* 38:16-25.)

Jesus is the name of the love of God, a love that eternally dies for man. Truly to pronounce his name—and for the radical Christian the names of Jesus and God are ultimately one—is to participate in God's death in Jesus and thereby to know the God who *is* Jesus as the expanding or forward-moving process who is becoming "One Man."

III

God and History

I. DIALECTIC AND THEOLOGY

TODAY THE Christian theologian is faced with the primary problem of the identity of the Word that is present in our history. Insofar as the theologian recognizes the truth that ours is not simply a distinct moment of history but, rather, a moment or an era which is being born at the inevitable cost of the loss of its roots in a previous history, he can no longer search for the presence of the Word by means of a theology whose form and language was evolved in a now long distant past. We can sense the estrangement of the contemporary Christian from his own theological heritage by simply noting the inability of all traditional forms of theology to speak in the presence of our history. As the historical world of Christendom sinks ever more deeply into the darkness of an irrecoverable past, theology is faced with the choice either of relapsing into a dead and archaic language or of evolving a whole new form of speech. Already we have noted that the radical Christian has created a new language of faith, a language often purporting to be the expression of a final age of the Spirit; but now we must attempt a more direct appropriation of this language into the mode of an openly theological discourse. Immediately we must confess that to the extent that theology absorbs the radical Christian vision it will lose its traditional identity and appearance. Not only will each of its former categories be negated or transformed by this encounter, but so likewise the very method of theological thinking must be given a new direction and form.

Almost invariably the radical Christian has set himself against theology, believing that theology is inevitably bound to the authority of the Church, and thus is incapable either of speaking the original language of faith or of expressing a contemporary Christian vision. Quite simply the radical Christian has judged theology as such to be closed to either original thinking or imaginative vision, and the so-called renaissance of theology in the twentieth century has done little to dissipate the force of this judgment. Nevertheless, the fact remains that so long as the radical vision remains unassimilated by theological discourse it will both continue to remain foreign to the community of faith and appear to be confined to a peculiarly speculative or imaginative realm. The task of theology today is to appropriate a contemporary Christian vision in such a manner as to make it thinkable as faith. So far from continuing to find its ground in the finality of Biblical revelation, theology must seek contemporary expressions of the Word of faith, opening itself to the address of a Word that has become fully actual in the present, an incarnate Word that has ceased to be meaningful and real in its original or initial expression. Above all, theology must abandon a religious form, wholly and consistently repudiating the religious quest for the primordial sacred, and with it the religious negation and reversal of the profane; for to the extent that theology even now remains bound to a primordial or transcendent Word it will remain closed to the present and human actuality of history. Consequently, theology must follow the radical Christian in passing through the death of God, in dying to every echo and memory of the reality of the primordial God, not as a means of simply capitulating to its own dissolution, but rather as a way to the rebirth of itself.

We have seen that radical faith envisions a moving Word or Spirit, a Word becoming embodied in the actual process of history in such a way as to lose or negate its original and earlier forms, thereby undergoing a real metamorphosis or transformation. Insofar as this movement entails a progressive negation of the original identity of Spirit, it is a dialectical movement, a movement whereby Spirit actually becomes its own other. A theological thinking which would capture the meaning of this movement must inevitably be dialectical, expressing in its own form and language the dynamic process of the metamorphosis of the Incarnate Word: for when theology is bound to an abstract and impassive Word, it must betray the historical reality of the Incarnation. Moreover, it is of vital importance to note that when theology has been purely theological in a strict and limited sense, that is to say when it has limited itself to an abstract and conceptual understanding of God himself, it has not only been nondialectical but it has also been estranged from both the original language of Biblical faith as well as the contemporary language of Christian witness and proclamation. Until the nineteenth century, dialectical thinking had only decisively entered into Christian theology at two points, in the Augustinian conception of nature and grace, and in the Lutheran understanding of law and gospel. Both of these achievements of Christian dialectical theology were Biblical and contemporary at once: they built upon a genuine Biblical ground while being expressions of a new historical movement of faith, and each prepared the way for a new and even revolutionary Christian era. Let us also note that these theological movements were grounded in a new understanding of the Incarnation, a new response to the forward movement of the Christian Word; and each in its own way effected or recorded a negation and transcendence of the eternal and primordial reality of God. Augustine's conception of the omnipresence and the omnipotence of grace proceeded out of a dialectical negation and reversal of the ontological givenness of Being, just as Luther's understanding of the free gift of grace in Christ rested upon an abridgment or annulment of the transcendent distance and the sovereign authority of the Creator. In either case, we find a new and more comprehensive form of the uniquely Christian Word, a form evolving out of a negation or transformation of the original or religious form of God.

Yet neither Augustine nor Luther reached a fully comprehensive and consistent mode of dialectical understanding, each remained bound to past and heteronomous norms of the Church—ironically, both Augustine and Luther demonically deepened those norms when they encountered other radical expressions of faith—and neither was able to bridge the gulfs established by the dualistic and nondialectical tendencies of their own thinking. If only because Augustinianism and Lutheranism remained dualistic, being unable to accept the full implications of their own movements of dialectical negation—for Augustine isolated the omnipotence of God from the omnipotence of grace, just as Luther isolated law from gospel—both finally sanctioned the primordial sacrality of God. Augustine and Luther have often been criticized as nonsystematic thinkers, but from a dialectical point of view, what this judgment really means is that neither was able to truly escape from the abstract and formal categories of a purely rational thinking; for Augustine remained a neoplatonist despite the fact that he had effected a transformation of Greek philosophical thinking, and the Luther who could so violently condemn the "whore reason" nevertheless was unable to break with the rational necessity of the unchanging identity of God. When Christian theology so binds itself to the abstract and static categories of our dominant Western logic, it can be open neither to the real and dynamic movement of the Word nor to a metamorphosis of a primordial Word in the actuality of history. For so long as theological thinking is grounded in the logical laws of identity and contradiction it cannot apprehend a forward-moving and self-transfiguring Word, and must simply submit to the ever-widening gulf between the primordial God and an increasingly profane and actual historicity. Hegel, who wrote the first and greatest Western dialectical treatise on logic, insisted that it is only when dialectical understanding (*Vernunft*) has negated and transcended the logical laws of pure reason (*Verstand*), that thinking can apprehend the movement of Spirit in history. Thus he declared that all actual or living beings are contradictory in themselves, and therefore contradiction is more real than a seemingly unchanging identity: "For as opposed to it identity is only the determination of the simple immediate, or of dead Being, while contradiction is the root of all movement and life, and it is only insofar as it contains contradiction that anything moves and has impulse and activity" (*Logic,* Vol. I, Bk. II, Sec. I, Ch. 3).

Dialectically considered, perhaps the most demonic consequence of a theology that accepts as its foundation the primordial sovereignty and holiness of God is its submission to the providential authority of what Hegel called the "Given," or that which happens to appear or to be at hand. Throughout the nineteenth century, radical Christians such as Dostoevsky violently protested against a theodicy that would sanction every horror and injustice in the name of the absolute sovereignty of God. For the simple truth is that so long as God is known only in his primordial form there lies no way to a theological understanding of history, for either history is totally negated following the universal religious way or it is ruthlessly subordinated to the alien authority of what Luther called the "law" or Blake names as Urizen ("your reason"). Just as a purely abstract and formal reason reflects the unchanging givenness of the world, the God of religion is impassive and immobile, and must inevitably appear in history as the enemy of movement and life. When Nietzsche understood the Christian God as the deepest embodiment of man's self-hatred and resentment, he unveiled the solitary and transcendent God of Christianity as the absolute antithesis of a total existence in history or what the new Zarathustra calls the "body." It is precisely because a primordial and religious deity is the antithesis of life and history that its sacred name can so naturally and spontaneously be evoked to sanction evil and injustice (e.g., The Book of Job). No horror in our history has been too great for it not to be embraced by the majority of the theological spokesmen who speak in its presence, for all historical as opposed to mythological witness to the primordial deity necessarily directs itself against the dynamic movement and the human actuality of history. What greater theological consistency could we expect than for a theologian who speaks for the primordial God to speak in the name of everything that confines and constricts the human hand and face?

A Christian dialectical theology must direct itself to an understanding of a Word that is penetrating the present, or a transcendent Word becoming immanent, and therefore it must speak against both the ecclesiastical norms of the past and all that reality which is alien and repressive in the present. Above all, such a theology must assault every source of meaning that lies beyond or stands opposed to the life and movement of humanity, attacking the ultimate barriers to the expansion of humanity, insofar as these appear to be rooted in an eternal and unchanging ground. So far from being the servant of the dogmatic and institutional authority of the Church, a truly dialectical theology will dissolve all such authority, and give itself to an attack upon every repressive law and power that claims a holy or a transcendent source. Whether in East or West, dialectical thinking has ever set itself against all forms of dualism, discovering an infallible sign of inhuman repression or willful illusion in every ultimate distinction between two realms of meaning or reality, if only because all such distinctions foreclose the possibility of the realization of the total rebirth or transfiguration of humanity. Only a false dialectic posits an ultimate and irreconcilable chasm between the opposites, for to the extent that the opposites are dualistically isolated from one another they are frozen in a static form and denied their own intrinsic resolution.

Certainly no Christian or incarnational theology can submit to a final and absolute opposition between time and Eternity or the finite and the infinite: for such an opposition simply reflects an abstract, an unmoving, or a primordial Word, in short, a Word that cannot become incarnate. Furthermore, a theology positing an absolute distinction between man and God, or the creature and the Creator, has no basis for seeking the total presence of the Word; it must cling to the transcendent and wholly other God, refusing the kenotic movement and epiphany of Christ, thereby denying the historical reality of the Incarnation.

Once theology accepts a fully dialectical vocation, it will negate its inherited categories insofar as these are given an unchanging identity, recognizing that dialectically the opposites pass into one another, and therefore the language of theology must undergo a continuous metamorphosis if it is to reflect the kenotic and historical movement of the Christian Word. A dynamic and forward-moving Word or Spirit can only partially and provisionally be recorded by a particular idea or image: that idea or image must in turn negate itself in response to the movement of the Word, and theological thinking must progressively lose its original form if it is to apprehend the increasingly universal epiphany of Spirit. If theology is a living discipline, a mode of understanding evolving with the movement of its historical ground and source, then it must understand that it can retain its traditional identity only by renouncing the Incarnate Word. To confine theological meaning to the sacred history and scriptures of the past is to abjure the activity of the Word in the present and to reverse the kenotic direction of the uniquely Christian Word. Moreover, the eschatological goal of the original and the authentic Christian Word demands that it be an activity or a process of making all things new, of transforming the totality of history so that God may be all in all, therewith annulling all that distance separating the creature and the Creator, and obliterating every opposition between the sacred and the profane, or flesh and Spirit. Yet, as we have seen, if such a process is to be active and real, it must be a process of Spirit actually becoming flesh and of flesh actually becoming Spirit: only a real and forward-moving process of Spirit becoming its own other can culminate in an apocalyptic *coincidentia oppositorum.*

Nothing less is demanded of contemporary theology than that it open itself to the meaning of an apocalyptic and total redemption, a redemption issuing from the total presence of God in Christ, as God himself becomes the Word who is progressively incarnate in the actual processes of history. A theology expressing the incarnate movement of God must negate its image of the primordial God, closing itself to every echo and memory of God's original form so as to open itself to the metamorphosis of God's original sacrality and transcendence in a profane and immanent totality. Dialectically, everything depends upon recognizing the meaning of God's total identification with Jesus and of understanding that it is God who becomes Jesus and not Jesus who becomes God. The forward movement of the Incarnate Word is from God to Jesus, and the Word continues its kenotic movement and direction by moving from the historical Jesus to the universal body of humanity, thereby undergoing an epiphany in every human hand and face. At no point in this dialectical process can we isolate the Word and affirm that here it receives its final and definitive expression. Any such abstraction of the Word from history must necessarily lose the meaning of an incarnational process, isolating theology from the activity and movement of the Word, and inevitably setting theology upon the retrogressive path of the religious forms of Christianity. Thus, regression must be identified as the intrinsic enemy of the Christian faith; it is the supreme temptation of a faith that celebrates the forward movement of the Word, and theology must ever give itself to a negation of every past form of the Word, if only as a means of opening itself to an extension of an eschatological future into the present.

II. THE CHRISTIAN NAME OF GOD

From the point of view of a radical and dialectical Christian theology, the absolutely decisive and fundamental theological principle is that the God of faith so far from being unchanging and unmoving is a perpetual and forward-moving process of self-negation, pure negativity, or kenotic metamorphosis. A consistent and fully dialectical form of radical Christianity cannot know an eternal and primordial God who forever remains bound to his original identity, if only because radical faith is a total response to the actual presence and the forward movement of God in history. Therefore, radical faith must negate the primordial name and image of God if it is to respond to the real movement of God himself. As opposed to a purely religious form of faith with its backward movement of involution and return, a distinctively Christian form of faith must ever be open to new epiphanies of the Word or Spirit of God, epiphanies that will not simply be repetitions of the original manifestation of God, or even ever more comprehensive illuminations of his eternal glory and power but, rather, truly new epiphanies whose very occurrence either effects or records a new actualization or movement of the divine process. Insofar as Christian theology has almost invariably assumed a priestly form—i.e., has been directed to a recovery or re-presentation of the original Word of faith—it has been grounded in a religious conception of the Creator or the God of the Beginning and closed to an understanding of the eschatological Christ of the End. Quite naturally the God of Christian theology has been both estranged from the forward movement of faith and alien to the Word or Spirit that has progressively dawned in the profane movement of our history. Not until theology is able to understand the self-negation or self-transformation of

God himself will it be able to arrive at an eschatological conception of the actual and forward movement of God.

If we are to become open to a contemporary and authentically Christian name or epiphany of God, we must first repudiate all religious conceptions of the mystery of the Godhead, with their inevitable corollary that the sacred or ultimate Reality is impassive and silent, and thus incapable of moving or speaking in history. To say that the name of God is unutterable is not simply to renounce the God of the Bible but to follow a retrogressive path leading to a total rebellion against history and a consequent religious quest for the lost innocence of the primordial Beginning. Closely linked to this religious refusal of the name of God is the dogmatic insistence that the names or epiphanies of God have for once and for all occurred in the past, with the consequence that faith must ever be a recollection or remembrance of a past and eternally given form of God. When faith is so conceived as a process of recollection or remembrance not only must it be identified with a backward movement of return but it must also be set against the forward movement of history and the cosmos. We must take due note of the fact that it is the prophetic tradition, as recorded in the Old and New Testaments, and this tradition alone, which gives witness to the forward or progressive movement of revelation, a movement wherein the God of faith appears in new and ever more dynamic epiphanies, as the prophetic oracle actualizes the name of God in such a manner as to reveal the integral relation between the divine process and the human reality of history. The God of the Biblical prophetic tradition is a God who speaks or reveals himself in history; here history is not the passive receptacle of the divine speech, but is rather the arena in which that speech itself becomes actual and real: for apart from history God would be silent, impassive, and alone. By the very act of revealing his name, God empties himself of an original plenitude, negating the God who alone is God, the *causa sui,* the unmoved Mover who is the sole cause of himself.

At long last, theology must come to an understanding of the inevitable correlation between God's self-revelation and his self-negation or *kenōsis*. The God who reveals himself in history is the God who empties himself of the plenitude of his primordial Being; thereby he actually and truly becomes manifest in history, and finally history becomes not simply the arena of revelation but the very incarnate Body of God. Accordingly, revelation is here an actual movement from Beginning to End, a real and forward movement from the primordial Being of God to the God who becomes all in all in the End. Progressively but decisively God abandons or negates his original passivity and quiescence—and a knowledge of the primordial name and reality of God is present neither in the Bible nor in Christianity, but is fully manifest in the purest expressions of religion—becoming incarnate both *in* and *as* the actuality of world and history. Indeed, from the Christian point of view, revelation and incarnation are inseparable, being but two faces of a single process, a process wherein God both reveals himself in and becomes incarnate as the very opposite of his original identity. Revelation, as it occurs in the Biblical prophetic tradition, gives witness to a fall or gradual dissolution of the primordial God, as God progressively becomes actualized and real in history, finally dawning as an all-encompassing but immanent and imminent "Kingdom of God." Therefore, a consistent and radical Christianity will embody no knowledge of the primordial God but instead will incorporate and make real that "Kingdom of God" which is a consequence of the absolute self-negation of God.

If radical Christianity disembodies the primordial God, refusing even the name of the sovereign Creator, then a new or radical theology must seek an understanding of the uniquely Christian name of God, opening itself to a full theological understanding of the name of Jesus Christ. First, we must recognize that Jesus Christ is the name of the God who has become fully and totally incarnate, and thus it is a divine name, a name revealing the actual movement of God himself. The name of Jesus Christ is simply meaningless apart from its Old Testament background, for it is the God of the Old Testament who becomes fully actualized and historically real in Christ. When the Christian proclaims the Lordship of Jesus, he is speaking of that same God whom the Old Testament knows as Creator, Lawgiver, and Lord; but here an originally sovereign and transcendent God appears in a totally empty or kenotic form. Moreover, it is only through faith in Christ that the believer can know the Old Testament names of God as epiphanies of God's self-negation or emptying of himself. If it is true to say that only the Biblical tradition knows the God who is the absolutely sovereign Creator and the wholly other Lawgiver and Judge, then the Christian, even as Job, must come to know the Creator and Judge as an alien and even self-estranged epiphany of God. Only an alien or empty form of God could be wholly other than man and the world, for the God whose very reality and power crushes the spirit of man is a God who is estranged from his own identity as Redeemer. The El Shaddai or almighty Lord who reveals himself to Job as the absolutely sovereign Creator is a God who is estranged from his own acts of redemption: thus an impassable gulf appears between man and God at precisely that point when God ceases to exist and to act in his redemptive form. The theologian may well speak of a divine economy of salvation, a process of history wherein man and God, or world and deity, become manifest and real in new forms or manifestations; and obviously the relation between man and God must undergo genuine transformations as this process unfolds. Yet if this process is actual and real, that is to say if it is a historical process occurring in the concrete contingencies of time and space, then God himself must act and exist in such a manner as to negate his primordial mode of Being.

Hegel, ever the dialectical thinker, maintains that Spirit has real or actual existence only insofar as it alienates itself from itself, and therefore Spirit can only move forward by a process of self-estrangement or self-negation. God moves forward in history by negating his present and previous modes of Being; only insofar as he ceases to act and exist in a given manifestation does God evolve to a new form, as his progressive historical epiphany carries him farther and farther away from his primordial or prehistoric identity. Nevertheless, it is crucial to maintain that God remains God or the divine process remains itself even while in a state of self-estrangement. Indeed, the Christian confesses that God is most truly or actually himself while in a state of ultimate self-alienation or self-estrangement. For the Christian believes that God most fully reveals himself in Jesus Christ: and the kenotic acts of the Incarnation and the Crucifixion are by no means to be understood as fragmentary epiphanies of the power and glory of an eternal and unchanging Godhead, but rather as historical acts or events whereby the Godhead finally ceases to exist and to be real in its past and primordial manifestations. If a radical monotheism is present only in the Biblical tradition, or if it is only here that God remains himself in a diverse and ever more actual series of historical epiphanies, then the Christian alone knows the God who remains God in a total act of self-estrangement or self-emptying. The Christian name of God is the name of a process of absolute self-negation, as God reveals himself in Jesus Christ to be the God who has come and freely died for man.

When the Christian proclaims Jesus Christ as the triumphant epiphany of God, he is not speaking of an epiphany of glory and power; or, rather, power and glory here pass into the opposite of their original manifestation, as God now appears and is real only in an absolute act of self-sacrifice or self-negation. Yet Jesus Christ is the consummation of the historical acts and movements of God: the forward-moving process and kenotic energy of God have ever evolved through sacrificial acts of self-negation, as God has acted to estrange himself from his own original Totality, thereby making possible an actual movement to a new and wholly other Totality of the End. A century and a half of historical scholarship has demonstrated that the Bible contains a diverse body or series of traditions and imagery that resists all theological attempts at harmonization or reconciliation. No longer is it possible to speak of a Biblical faith or a Biblical religion or even of a distinct and singular Biblical God; nor is there any possibility of rationally or logically uniting the self-contradictory Biblical images of God. Nevertheless, a radical and dialectical theology can lead us to grasp the necessity of the contradictory language of the Bible. Here alone we can come to understand the meaning of a divine process progressively moving through a self-negation of an original ground to new and ever more opposing epiphanies, as these epiphanies continually oppose and reverse the primordialsacrality of God. Once we truly come to understand the Christian God as an actual and moving dialectical process, we shall finally be purged of the Christian religious belief in the existence of a unique and absolutely autonomous God.

What can it mean to speak of the Christian God as a dialectical process rather than as an existent Being? First, it means that the Christian God cannot be known as an unchanging, an unmoving, or an impassive Being; nor can he be understood as possessing a common nature or substance that remains eternally the same throughout his revelatory and redemptive acts. If the Christian knows the God who has emptied himself of his original sacrality in actually becoming flesh, then he cannot know a God who remains distinct and self-enclosed in his own primordial Being. The God who acts in the world and history is a God who negates himself, gradually but decisively annihilating his own original Totality. God is that Totality which "falls" or "descends," thereby moving ever more fully into the opposite of its original identity. God or the Godhead becomes the God who is manifest in Christ by passing through a reversal of His original form: thus transcendence becomes immanence just as Spirit becomes flesh. At no point in this process is God uniquely himself: each point or moment in the process embodies a metamorphosis of God, as God remains himself even while estranged from himself, for it is precisely God's self-estrangement or self-negation that actualizes his forward movement and process. True, the Christian proclaims the God who has totally negated or sacrificed himself in Christ. Yet the Christian confesses that it is God who has become Christ; and the God who became Christ was once manifest and real as Creator and Lord. Otherwise, it is not possible to speak of the kenotic Christ, or of the self-annihilation of God, or of God as having actually negated himself in Jesus Christ. Therefore, to speak of God as a dialectical process rather than as an existent Being is to speak of the God who has emptied himself of God in Christ.

The Christian who comes to understand God as a kenotic and forward-moving process will be delivered from the temptation to think of God as a wholly other and autonomous Being just as he will be freed from any form of theological dualism. Nondialectical expressions of Christianity have by one means or another invariably established a chasm between the essential or integral reality of God and his redemptive and revelatory acts. When God has been known apart from his acts, the path of natural or rational theology, then a breach is established between the God of faith and the God of the understanding, a breach reflecting an internal bifurcation between the activity of the mind and the life of faith. On the other hand, any attempt to limit the meaning of God to the Word of his revelation must not only abandon all cognitive and imaginative meanings of God but must also isolate the reality of God from the reality of the world, therewith isolating God from both the arena and the actuality of his acts. Both natural and revealed theology refuse the full reality of God: the one conceiving a primordial or eternal nature of God that is incapable of either forward movement or redemptive action, and the other positing a sovereign Lord who is infinitely removed from the immediate or historical reality of his creation. Yet most damning of all, both the dogmatic expressions of revealed theology and the established forms of philosophical theology isolate God from Christ, establishing an unbridgeable chasm between the Creator and the Redeemer, or the primordial and the consequent natures of God, thus finally regressing to pagan or religious forms of Christianity.

Blake ingeniously sensed that the God of deism and the God of orthodoxy are identical, for both banish the redemptive God from the world, and in positing God as either the impassive source of cosmic order or the tyrannical despot of history arrive at a common conception of a distant and alien God. Indeed, as historical or ecclesiastical Christianity has progressively regressed from its original faith it has deepened the chasm between the Creator and the Redeemer, until in our time a redemptive meaning of God has wholly vanished. To reverse this process of regression we must return to the fundamental principle of dialectical theology: God is a forward-moving process of kenotic metamorphosis who remains himself even while passing through a movement of absolute self-negation. "God is Jesus," cries Blake and every radical Christian seer, because God himself has become incarnate and is fully and totally identical with Christ. So likewise we must resist every Gnostic and dualistic temptation to split asunder the Creator and the Redeemer by recognizing that if God is identical with Christ, then Christ is the final embodiment of God's self-negation. At no point is the Gospel of John more anti-Gnostic than in its attempt to portray Christ as the Creator, for the almighty Creator who became Christ is already in his original act and epiphany the God who is capable of emptying himself of his sovereign power. Dialectically considered, every act of God is a kenotic metamorphosis, for the God who acts as the Creator is a God who has fallen from an original Totality, and even the most awesome and oppressive acts of God can be understood by the Christian as preparations for the gospel. Nevertheless, the Christian must betray his faith if he refuses the forward movement of the divine process. God negates himself as sovereign Creator in becoming incarnate in Christ: God as Creator and Lord undergoes a metamorphosis in Christ, so that he passes into the opposite of his original epiphany. Christ is identical with God, yes, but the God who is present and real in Christ is the God who has emptied himself of his original sovereignty and transcendence. Hence the Christian who lives in Christ must refuse every image of the preincarnate God except insofar as such images are transfigured by the self-sacrifice or self-negation of God himself.

III. GOD AND SATAN

While inquiring, in *The Genealogy of Morals,* into man's employment of God as an instrument of his own self-torture, Nietzsche remarks that man projected all his denials of self and nature out of himself as God: "as transcendence, as eternity, as endless torture, as hell, as the infinitude of guilt and punishment." These words repeat in their own distinctive way Blake's prophetic attack upon Urizen and Hegel's dialectical assault upon an alien and lifeless form of Spirit. Moreover, they illuminate a uniquely Christian epiphany of God: the God who is infinitely distant from man, the God who in his transcendent majesty stands over against man, and before whom man is reduced to an abject condition of guilt and dread. Why is it that historians of religion have failed to note that Rudolf Otto's idea of the numinous as *mysterium tremendum et fascinans* is drawn from the Christian vision of God and is exemplified nowhere else in the world's religions? Not even the Muslim or the Jew (except for a modern and semi-Christianized Jew such as Kafka) knows a deity whose very sacrality is absolutely opposed to the life and immediacy of man's existence in the world. Nor does the Muslim or the Jew—to say nothing of the participants in the mystical ways of the East—know that awesome and overwhelming guilt deriving from a naked encounter with a divine and righteous Judge. Melville's portrait of Moby Dick, just as Ivan Karamazov's rebellion against God, has inevitably cast a spell upon the modern Christian; because only the modern Christian has known a God who appears only as *mysterium tremendum,* the awesome Lord whose sovereign power annuls the energy and movement of humanity.

Let us return to those prophetic words of Nietzsche unveiling Christianity as the absolute form of self-negation:

> The Christian conception of God—God as god of the sick, God as a spider, God as spirit—is one of the most corrupt conceptions of the divine ever attained on earth. It may even represent the low-water mark in the descending development of divine types. God degenerated into the contradiction of life, instead of being its transfiguration and eternal Yes! God as the declaration of war against life, against nature, against the will to live! God—the formula for every slander against "this world," for every lie about the "beyond"! God—the deification of nothingness, the will to nothingness pronounced holy! (*The Antichrist,* Section 18.)

Note that Nietzsche understands the Christian conception of God as reflecting the lowest point in a descending series of divine epiphanies. Who can doubt, particularly in view of Nietzsche's praise of the earliest Old Testament images of Yahweh as the expression of Israel's original consciousness of power and joy and hope, that here he is speaking in the context of the forward movement of Biblical prophetic revelation, a movement wherein God progressively appears as the apocalyptic God of the End, a God whose final epiphany must bring an end to the values and reality of the world? When Nietzsche speaks of the Christian God as the deification of nothingness, he is speaking of that primal Christian vision of God which apprehends an absolute polarity between God and the world. The Christian God is the contradiction of life because here God finally appears and is real in his divine form as an infinitely sovereign power that crushes the life of man. But in what sense may we say that the Christian God is the will to nothingness pronounced holy? Do we not perceive a far holier will to nothingness in the Buddhist? Yet the Buddhist is liberated from an abstract and empty nothingness, the nothingness of a fragmentary and isolated selfhood, by a realization of Nirvana or Sunyata: that all-encompassing, blissful, and total nothingness which appears precisely at the point where an empty nothingness is dissolved. Whereas, on the contrary, the Christian God may only truly be known by an absolute negation of the fullness of life and the flesh, a negation inverting the energy and joy of the body.

Accordingly, the Christian God is the deepest embodiment of Nietzsche's symbol of No-saying, that absolute life and self-negation which finally turns upon itself. Once again, however, we are being led by another route to the divine process of self-negation. If God truly negates or sacrifices himself, then his alien and empty form is an inevitable consequence of his own act of self-negation, and thence God himself can only be present or real in his divine form as the absolute antithesis of life and energy. Consequently, only the Christian can know the God who is Wholly Other, for only a life in Christ can make real the fruits of God's self-negation, and therein actualize or make historically present the now lifeless body or actual emptiness of the God who has died in Christ. From this point of view, we can see that Christendom's progressive movement away from the presence of a redemptive epiphany of God is a historical actualization of its original roots. The God who is finally manifest in Christian experience as the divine Judge and Executioner, or known as an abstract and totally lifeless Being, is the God who is the historical consequence of the divine process of kenotic metamorphosis. In one sense, the kenotic movement of the Incarnation reaches its consummation when God finally appears in human experience as the contradiction of life and the deification of nothingness. The totally alien God, a God already foreseen by Gnosticism, is simply the dead body of God, a body that only gradually decomposes in the history of Christendom, being known at first in conjunction with its preincarnate and living form, but increasingly revealing its life-negating emptiness, until with the disintegration of Christendom, it is finally actualized in history as the total embodiment of an alien and empty nothingness.

Although a terrifying experience of awe and dread in response to an epiphany of the Creator is already recorded in The Book of Job, it is not until the advent of the modern world that we may discover a pervading and comprehensive sense of dread, a dread or *Angst* that Kierkegaard truly named as the product of an encounter with nothingness. Pascal shuddered at the vast stretches of an infinite and empty space, but now that shudder is potentially present wherever the human heart is still capable of opening itself to what has increasingly become the brute facticity or the radical finitude of the world. The modern Christian seer, whether a Blake or a Nietzsche, has proclaimed that the chaos lying upon our horizon is a nothingness evolving from the death of God, the tomb of the dead Creator. Thus Nietzsche's Madman, in announcing the death of God, unveils an earth that is unchained from its sun:

> Whither is it moving now? Whither are we moving now? Away from all suns? Are we not plunging continually? Backward, sideward, forward, in all directions? Is there any up or down left? Are we not straying as through an

infinite nothing? Do we not feel the breath of empty space? Has it not become colder? Is not night and more night coming on all the while? Must not lanterns be lit in the morning? Do we not hear anything yet of the noise of the gravediggers who are burying God? Do we not smell anything yet of God's decomposition? Gods too decompose. God is dead.

Immersed as we are in the new chaos released by the death of the Creator, we have seemingly lost Adam's capacity for naming the creation, as faith becomes mute in face of a wholly alien and exterior cosmos. But it does not remain mute if it can name our chaos as the tomb of God. Neither will dread immobilize the Christian who comes to recognize our *Angst* as the "smell" of God's decomposition. For to know an alien and empty nothingness as the dead body of God is to be liberated from every uncanny and awesome sense of the mystery and power of chaos.

Remarkably enough, a comparable victory over chaos is present in an earlier apocalyptic faith, as the apocalyptic believer comes to know the world as an "old aeon" which even now is returning to chaos, and thus coming to an end. Almost certainly it was apocalyptic religion, probably in its original Persian expression, which first evolved a belief in Satan or Antichrist, a cosmic and historical power of evil and nothingness that is the polar opposite of a beneficent Creator. Not only is Satan here known as ruling over the world throughout the downward path of history, but he is the ultimate author of evil, and in later Gnostic and Catholic theology he is conceived as the very embodiment of nothingness. Not until Satan or Antichrist has been conquered will the triumph of the "new aeon" be realized, and with the defeat of Satan the "old aeon" passes away or wholly relapses into nothingness. When Jesus sees Satan falling from heaven, he knows that the time is at hand for the dawning of the Kingdom of God. Just as the "new aeon" arises out of the ashes of a disintegrating world of darkness, the Kingdom of God which

Jesus proclaims reverses the values and institutions of history, bringing an end to the foundation of all tyrannical and repressive power. The reversal of that power marks the fall of Satan: for Satan is the power enclosing energy and stilling movement, the power of darkness standing over against and opposing all life and light. According to ancient apocalyptic writings, Satan or Antichrist only openly appears in history at the moment of his fall: not until the advent of the time of his dissolution is it possible to unveil or name the Antichrist. Apocalyptic seers have ever attempted the naming of Antichrist, commonly veiling their attempts in esoteric symbolisms, but throughout the history of Christendom apocalyptic visions have ever remained bound to that mystery which the "new aeon" promises to bring to an end. Only with the collapse of Christendom does an apocalyptic seer appear who finally vanquishes the mystery of religion by unveiling the Christian God as Satan.

William Blake is that seer and we must fully acknowledge that Blake commits the blasphemy of blasphemies by identifying the Biblical Creator and Lord as Satan. Not only did Blake leave numerous personal statements to this effect but in his supreme pictorial creation, his illustrations to The Book of Job, he depicted God as Satan on the magnificent eleventh plate, and did so in fulfillment of his vision in this work that redemption can only fully be actualized after the transcendent and numinous God has undergone a cosmic and historical epiphany as Satan. This identification of God and Satan is a consistent motif throughout Blake's later work and it serves as the foundation of the apocalyptic vision of *Milton* and *Jerusalem*. In *Milton*, Satan has taken on all of the former functions of Urizen, only here Satan does not declare, "I am God alone" until he establishes the "Law" of repression (9:25). Remembering that *Milton* is Blake's vision of the apocalyptic regeneration of Christianity, we cannot fail to observe that here Satan is revealed as the "Shadow" or

"Spectre" of a fallen humanity, an empty chaos confining the energy of life, and constricting the movement of every human hand and face.

> And the Mills of Satan were separated into a moony Space
> Among the rocks of Albion's Temples, and Satan's Druid sons
> Offer the Human Victims throughout all the Earth, and Albion's
> Dread Tomb, immortal on his Rock, overshadow'd the whole Earth,
> Where Satan, making to Himself Laws from his own identity,
> Compell'd others to serve him in moral gratitude & submission,
> Being call'd God, setting himself above all that is called God;
> And all the Spectres of the Dead, calling themselves Sons of God,
> In his Synagogues worship Satan under the Unutterable Name.
>
> *(Milton* 11:6-14)

The synagogues to which Blake refers are the Christian churches, and the "Unutterable Name" is the name of the Christian God, whom Blake dares to name as the ultimate author of all sacrifice and the tyrannical ruler of a repressed and enslaved humanity.

"I am not a God afar off," declares the Savior in *Jerusalem* (4:18), but the Jesus who is present in the midst of life is the Word made flesh, the Word which has finally and totally descended from the transcendent realm of Spirit. Once this descent has taken place, the life and movement of the Word are no longer present in a transcendent beyond, and thereby all preincarnate epiphanies of the Word are emptied of their redemptive potency, and become reduced to alien and repressive powers. As Blake declares:

> Seek not thy heavenly father then beyond the
> skies,
> There Chaos dwells & ancient Night & Og & Anak
> old.
> For every human heart has gates of brass & bars
> of adamant
> Which few dare unbar, because dread Og & Anak
> guard the gates
> Terrific: and each mortal brain is wall'd and
> moated round
> Within, and Og & Anak watch here: here is the
> Seat
> Of Satan in its Webs.
>
> (*Milton* 20:32-38)

Og was a powerful Canaanite king who was defeated by the early Israelites, and the Anak were a gigantic people who were exterminated by Joshua; but Blake employs their names symbolically to speak of a resurrected chaos which returns with Satan's fall from heaven, and is present wherever Satan's "Web of Religion" binds life and energy to the laws of his own identity. Thus, too, religion only becomes repressive when it arises in response to the kenotic movement of the Incarnation, regressing to a now empty and alien form of Spirit by binding itself to that dead body of God which Blake names as Satan.

Karl Barth was the first theologian to maintain that the "secret" of the creation can only truly be known by faith in Christ. This all too modern motif is one of the most powerful themes of the *Church Dogmatics,* and it beautifully illustrates the quandary of the modern theologian who is forced to speak about God in a world in which God is dead. Thus, we need not doubt that even a priestly theology can speak the words of the gospel, particularly when these are interpreted from the point of view of the radical prophetic vision. One of Blake's more elusive visions apprehends Satan in the form of the Creator; but his epiphany as the Creator occurs precisely to the extent that his beholder becomes enslaved to his divine if empty center:

So spoke the Spectre to Albion: he is the Great
  Selfhood,
Satan, Worshipp'd as God by the Mighty Ones of
  the Earth,
Having a white Dot call'd a Center, from which
  branches out
A Circle in continual gyrations: this became a
  Heart
From which sprang numerous branches varying
  their motions,
Producing many Heads, three or seven or ten, &
  hands & feet
Innumerable at will of the unfortunate contempla-
  tor
Who becomes his food: such is the way of the
  Devouring Power.

                              (*Jerusalem* 33:17-24)

Notice the traditional images of the center and the circle, commonly employed to envision the all-encompassing power of God, but here the circle progressively moves out from the center in such a manner as to consume or annihilate all that space which it encompasses. One is reminded of Blake's early vision of Urizen as the Creator, who, unseen and unknown, divides and measures space by forming it in the image of his "ninefold darkness" (the first chapter of *The Book of Urizen*). We must not, however, imagine that such images simply testify to a Gnostic hatred of the world. They are, rather, violent reactions against a human world of alienation and repression, and they attempt to reveal the ultimate ground of the bondage of humanity, by seeking that ground in the walls or boundaries surrounding the arena of human existence.

"They became what they beheld," is a frequent refrain in *Jerusalem,* which is implicitly present in the text just cited: for to know the distant and almighty Creator is to submit to a creaturely status, a mode of existence wherein the creature is totally subordinate to the Creator, and therein enclosed within a microcosmic center. We truly recognize that alien Creator by faith in Christ because the God who has become Christ has liberated humanity from a distant heaven by annihilating the power and the movement of transcendent Spirit. When the Word becomes flesh, it ceases to be active and real in its original epiphany, and its preincarnate form thereby becomes lifeless and immobile, gradually regressing to a formless state of an abstract and empty nothingness. Yet a fallen humanity must inevitably know this nothingness as an all-encompassing and "Devouring Power," if only because a broken and shrunken humanity can only submit to its own microcosmic alienation and isolation from life and energy by imagining its macrocosmic boundaries as that infinite distance separating the creature and the Creator. Hence, as Nietzsche says, man projects all his denials of self and nature out of himself as God. The Christian God is the embodiment of an absolute No-saying because it is the only epiphany of the sacred which is a total reversal of a forward-moving divine process. Thus the Christian God can be manifest and real only by means of a faith engaging in an absolute world and life-negation, a negation that must occur wherever there is energy and life. When the radical Christian confronts us with the liberating message that God is Satan, he is stilling the power of that negation, breaking all those webs of religion with which a regressive Christianity has ensnared the Christian, and unveiling the God who had died in Christ.

IV

The Self-Annihilation of God

I. THE DEATH OF GOD

WHAT CAN it mean to speak of the death of God? Indeed, how is it even possible to speak of the death of God, particularly at a time when the name of God would seem to be unsayable? First, we must recognize that the proclamation of the death of God is a Christian confession of faith. For to know that God is dead is to know the God who died in Jesus Christ, the God who passed through what Blake symbolically named as "Self-Annihilation" or Hegel dialectically conceived as the negation of negation. Only the Christian can truly speak of the death of God, because the Christian alone knows the God who negates himself in his own revelatory and redemptive acts. Just as a purely religious apprehension of deity must know a God who is transcendent and beyond, so likewise a purely rational and nondialectical conception of deity must know a God who is impassive and unmoving, or self-enclosed in his own Being. Neither the religious believer nor the nondialectical thinker can grasp the God whose actuality and movement derives from his own acts of self-negation. Thus it is only the radical, or the profane, or the nonreligious Christian who knows that God has ceased to be active and real in his preincarnate or primordial reality.

Nevertheless, it is essential that the radical Christian make clear what he means by his confession, eliminating so far as possible all that confusion and ambiguity arising from the language of the death of God, and clearly establishing both his Christian claim and his repudiation of all forms of religious Christianity. To confess the death of God is to speak of an actual and real event, not perhaps an event occurring in a single moment of time or history, but notwithstanding this reservation an event that has actually happened both in a cosmic and in a historical sense. There should be no confusion deriving from the mistaken assumption that such a confession refers to an eclipse of God or a withdrawal of God from either history or the creation. Rather, an authentic language speaking about the death of God must inevitably be speaking about the death of God himself. The radical Christian proclaims that God has actually died in Christ, that this death is both a historical and a cosmic event, and, as such, it is a final and irrevocable event, which cannot be reversed by a subsequent religious or cosmic movement. True, a religious reversal of the death of God has indeed occurred in history, is present in the religious expressions of Christianity, and is now receding into the mist of an archaic, if not soon to be forgotten, past. But such a religious reversal cannot annul the event of the death of God; it cannot recover the living God of the old covenant, nor can it reverse or bring to an end the progressive descent of Spirit into flesh. Religious Christians may know a resurrected Lord of the Ascension, just as they may be bound to an almighty and distant Creator and Judge. Yet such a flight from the finality of the Incarnation cannot dissolve the event of the Incarnation itself even if it must finally impel the Christian to seek the presence and the reality of Christ in a world that is totally estranged from Christianity's established vision of the sacred.

Once again we must attempt to draw a distinction between the original or primal death of God in Christ and the actualization or historical realization of his death throughout the whole gamut of human experience. Remembering the radical Christian affirmation that God has fully and totally become incarnate in Christ, we must note that neither the Incarnation nor the Crucifixion can here be understood as isolated and once-and-for-all events; rather, they must be conceived as primary expressions of a forward-moving and eschatological process of redemption, a process embodying a progressive movement of Spirit into flesh. At no point in this process does the incarnate Word or Spirit assume a final and definitive form, just as God himself can never be wholly or simply identified with any given revelatory event or epiphany, if only because the divine process undergoes a continual metamorphosis, ever moving more deeply and more fully toward an eschatological consummation. While the Oriental mystic knows an incarnational process whereby the sacred totally annihilates or transfigures the profane, a process providing us with our clearest image of the primordial reality of the sacred, it is Christianity alone which witnesses to a concrete and actual descent of the sacred into the profane, a movement wherein the sacred progressively abandons or negates its particular and given expressions, thereby emptying them of their original power and actuality. Radical Christianity knows this divine or incarnational process as a forward-moving Totality. Neither a primordial God nor an original garden of innocence remains immune to this process of descent: here all things whatsoever are drawn into and transfigured by this cosmic or total process of metamorphosis. This movement from "Innocence" to "Experience" is potentially or partially present at every point of time and space, and in every epiphany of the divine process: thus we could even say that God dies in some sense wherever he is present or actual in the world, for God actualizes himself by negating his original or given expressions. Yet we truly know this divine process of negativity only by knowing God's death in Christ.

Estranged as we are from our Christian heritage, and distant as we most certainly are from the actual faith of the earliest disciples, what can the contemporary Christian know of the original epiphany of God in Christ?

Initiated as we are, moreover, into a historical consciousness that has unveiled a whole new world of New Testament thought and imagery, a world that is subject neither
to theological systemization nor to translation into modern
thought and experience, how can we hope to ascertain
the fundamental meaning for us of the original Christian
faith? Let us openly confess that there is no possibility of
our returning to a primitive Christian faith, and that the
Christ who can become contemporary to us is neither the
original historical Jesus nor the Lord of the Church's
earliest proclamation. Given our historical situation in
the twilight of Christendom, we have long since died to
the possibility of a classical or orthodox Christian belief,
and must look upon both the New Testament and early
Christianity as exotic and alien forms of religion. Nevertheless, and here we continue to have much to learn from
the radical Christian, we cannot neglect the possibility that
it is precisely our alienation from the religious world of
primitive Christianity which can make possible our realization of the fundamental if underlying meaning of the earliest expressions of the Christian faith. For if a religious
movement necessarily embodies a backward movement of
involution and return, then the very fact that we have
died to the religious form of early Christianity can make
possible our passage through a reversal of religious Christianity, a reversal that can open to us a new and fuller
participation in the forward movement of the Incarnation.

We know that the proclamation of both Jesus and the
earliest Palestinian churches revolved about the announcement of the glad tidings or the gospel of the dawning of
the Kingdom of God. But thus far neither the theologian
nor the Biblical scholar has been able to appropriate the
eschatological symbol of the Kingdom of God in such a
manner as to make it meaningful to the modern consciousness without thereby sacrificing its original historical
meaning. It is scarcely questionable, however, that this
symbol originally pointed to the final consummation of a

dynamic process of the transcendent's becoming immanent: of a distant, a majestic, and a sovereign Lord breaking into time and space in such a way as to transfigure and
renew all things whatsoever, thereby abolishing the old
cosmos of the original creation, and likewise bringing to
an end all that law and religion which had thus far been
established in history. The very form of Christianity's
original apocalyptic proclamation rests upon an expecta-
tion that the actualization of the Kingdom of God will
make present not the almighty Creator, Lawgiver, and
Judge, but rather a wholly new epiphany of the deity, an
epiphany annihilating all that distance separating the creature from the Creator. Despite Paul's conviction that the
victory which Christ won over the powers of sin and darkness had annulled the old Israel and initiated the annihilation of the old creation, to say nothing of his assurance
that God will be all in all, both Paul and the early Church
were unable fully or decisively to negate the religious
forms of the old history, or to surmount their bondage to
the transcendent and primordial epiphany of God. Consequently, early Christianity was unable either to negate religion or to absorb and fully assimilate an apocalyptic
faith, with the result that it progressively became estranged
from its own initial proclamation.

Already we have seen that the modern radical Christian
has evolved an apocalyptic and dialectical mode of vision
or understanding revolving about an apprehension of the
death of God in Christ, and it is just this self-negation or
self-annihilation of the primordial reality of God which
actualizes the metamorphosis of an all-embracing Totality.
Can we not make the judgment that it is precisely this
vision of the death of God in Christ that can make possible
for us a realization of the deeper meaning of the Christian
and eschatological symbol of the dawning of the Kingdom
of God? Thereby we could know that the victory of the
Kingdom of God in Christ is the fruit of the final movement of God into the world, of Spirit into flesh, and that

the Christian meaning of the Kingdom of God is inseparable from an abolition or reversal of all those preincarnate forms or epiphanies of Spirit. By so conceiving the underlying meaning of the original Christian proclamation, we can also see that it is the religious vision of early Christianity which reverses the Christian reality of the Kingdom of God. Inevitably, the orthodox expressions of Christianity abandoned an eschatological ground, and no doubt the radical Christian's recovery of an apocalyptic faith and vision was in part occasioned by his own estrangement from the dominant and established forms of the Christian tradition. Such a contemporary appropriation of the symbol of the Kingdom of God can also make possible our realization of the gospel, or the "good news," of the death of God: for the death of God does not propel man into an empty darkness, it liberates him from every alien and opposing other, and makes possible his transition into what Blake hailed as "The Great Humanity Divine," or the final coming together of God and man.

Whether or not we choose to so understand the original Christian gospel of the dawning of the Kingdom of God, it is clear that the radical Christian affirms that God has died in Christ, and that the death of God is a final and irrevocable event. All too obviously, however, we cannot discover a clear and decisive witness to the meaning of this event in either the Bible or the orthodox teachings and visions of Christianity. But the radical Christian envisions a gradual and progressive metamorphosis of Spirit into flesh, a divine process continually negating or annihilating itself, as it ever moves forward to an eschatological goal. While the Christian proclaims that this process is triumphant in Christ, or that it is inaugurated in its final form by the events of the Incarnation and the Crucifixion, it does not follow that the process itself ceases to move forward in all that history following the death of Christ. Simply by noting the overwhelming power and the comprehensive expression of the modern Christian experience of the death of God, we can sense the effect of the ever fuller movement of the Word or Spirit into history, a movement whose full meaning only dawns with the collapse of Christendom, and in the wake of the historical realization of the death of God. A contemporary faith that opens itself to the actuality of the death of God in our history as the historical realization of the dawning of the Kingdom of God can know the spiritual emptiness of our time as the consequence in human experience of God's self-annihilation in Christ, even while recovering in a new and universal form the apocalyptic faith of the primitive Christian. Insofar as the kenotic or negative movement of the divine process is a movement into the actuality of human experience, it can neither be isolated in a given time and place nor be understood as wholly occurring within a given moment. On the contrary, the actualization of the metamorphosis of the Word into flesh is a continual and forward-moving process, a process initially occurring in God's death in Christ, yes, but a process that is only gradually and progressively realized in history, as God's original self-negation eventually becomes actualized throughout the total range of human experience.

Once again we have detected a Christian religious reversal of God's act in Christ: for a faith that isolates the sacred events of Christ's passion from the profane actuality of human experience must inevitably enclose Christ within a distant and alien form and refuse his presence in the immediacy of our existence. Every Christian attempt to create an unbridgeable chasm between sacred history and human history gives witness to a refusal of the Incarnation and a betrayal of the forward-moving process of salvation. We can discover a reversal of the kenotic movement of the Word in the very insistence of the religious Christian that faith has for once and for all been given, that it is fully and finally present in the Scriptures, the liturgies, the creeds, and the dogmas of the past, and can in no sense undergo a development or transformation that moves beyond its original expression to new and more universal forms. All such religious claims not only attempt to solidify and freeze the life and movement of the divine process, but they foreclose the possibility of the enlargement and evolution of faith, and ruthlessly set the believer against the presence of Christ in an increasingly profane history, thereby alienating the Christian from the actuality of his own time. The radical Christian calls upon his hearer to open himself to the fullness of our history, not with the illusory belief that our history is identical with the history that Jesus lived, but rather with the conviction that the death of God which has dawned so fully in our history is a movement into the total body of humanity of God's original death in Christ. Once we grasp the radical Christian truth that a radically profane history is the inevitable consummation of an actual movement of the sacred into the profane, then we can be liberated from every preincarnate form of Spirit, and accept our destiny as an occasion for the realization in the immediacy of experience of the self-emptying or self-annihilation of the transcendent and primordial God in the passion and death of Christ.

From this perspective it would even be possible to understand Christendom's religious reversal of the movement of Spirit into flesh as a necessary consequence of the Incarnation, preparing the way for a more comprehensive historical realization of the death of God by its progressive banishment of the dead body of God to an ever more transcendent and inaccessible realm. If we conceive of the Word or Spirit as moving more and more fully into the body of the profane in response to the self-negation of God in Christ, then we can understand how the Christian God gradually becomes more alien and beyond, receding into a lifeless and oppressive form, until it finally appears as an empty and vacuous nothingness. The God who is progressively manifest in human experience as an empty and alien other is the inevitable consequence of the Spirit who descends ever more deeply into flesh. Not only does the distant and alien God witness to the historical actualization of the Word in the flesh, but his epiphany as a vacuous and empty formlessness dissolves the possibility of a living and actual faith in God, thus impelling the Christian to seek a new epiphany of Christ in the world. Let the contemporary Christian rejoice that Christianity has evolved the most alien, the most distant, and the most oppressive deity in history: it is precisely the self-alienation of God from his original redemptive form that has liberated humanity from the transcendent realm, and made possible the total descent of the Word into the fullness of human experience. The God who died in Christ is the God who thereby gradually ceases to be present in a living form, emptying himself of his original life and power, and thereafter receding into an alien and lifeless nothingness.

The death of God in Christ is an inevitable consequence of the movement of God into the world, of Spirit into flesh, and the actualization of the death of God in the totality of experience is a decisive sign of the continuing and forward movement of the divine process, as it continues to negate its particular and given expressions, by moving ever more fully into the depths of the profane. A faith that knows this process as a self-negating and kenotic movement, as both embodied and symbolically enacted in the passion of Christ, knows that it becomes manifest in the suffering and the darkness of a naked human experience, an experience banished from the garden of innocence, and emptied of the sustaining power of a transcendent ground or source. So far from regarding the vacuous and rootless existence of modern man as the product of an abandonment of faith, the radical Christian recognizes the spiritual emptiness of our time as the historical actualization of the self-annihilation of God, and despite the horror and anguish embedded in such a condition of humanity, the radical Christian can greet even this darkness as a yet more comprehensive embodiment and fulfillment of the original passion of Christ.

Hence a radical faith claims our contemporary condition as an unfolding of the body of Christ, an extension into the fullness of history of the self-emptying of God. No evasion of an autonomous human condition is possible for the Christian who confesses his participation in a Word that has negated its primordial and transcendent ground: the Christian who lives in a fully incarnate Christ is forbidden either to cling to an original innocence or to yearn nostalgically for a preincarnate Spirit. Indeed, it is precisely the Christian's life in the kenotic Word which impels him to accept and affirm a world in which God is dead as the realization in history of God's self-annihilation in Christ.

Once the Christian has been liberated from all attachment to a celestial and transcendent Lord, and has died in Christ to the primordial reality of God, then he can say triumphantly: God is dead! Only the Christian can speak the liberating word of the death of God because only the Christian has died in Christ to the transcendent realm of the sacred and can realize in his own participation in the forward-moving body of Christ the victory of the self-negation of Spirit. Just as the primitive Christian could call upon his hearer to rejoice in the Crucifixion because it effected the advent of the Kingdom of God, the contemporary Christian can announce the glad tidings of the death of God, and speak with joy of the final consummation of the self-annihilation of God. True, every man today who is open to experience knows that God is absent, but only the Christian knows that God is dead, that the death of God is a final and irrevocable event, and that God's death has actualized in our history a new and liberated humanity. How does the Christian know that God is dead? Because the Christian lives in the fully incarnate body of Christ, he acknowledges the totality of our experience as the consummation of the kenotic passion of the Word, and by giving himself to the Christ who is present to us he is liberated from the alien power of an emptied and darkened transcendence. Rather than being mute and numb in response to the advent of a world in which the original name of God is no longer sayable, the Christian can live and speak by pronouncing the word of God's death, by joyously announcing the "good news" of the death of God, and by greeting the naked reality of our experience as the triumphant realization of the self-negation of God. What can the Christian fear of the power of darkness when he can name our darkness as the fulfillment of the self-emptying of God in Christ?

II. ATONEMENT

When the Incarnation and the Crucifixion are understood as dual expressions of a common process, a kenotic or negative process whereby God negates his primordial and transcendent epiphany thereby undergoing a metamorphosis into a new and immanent form, then the incarnate manifestation of Word or Spirit can also be understood as an eschatological consummation of the self-negation of God, an extension of the atoning process of the self-annihilation of God throughout the totality of experience. Such an apocalyptic and dialectical understanding of the atonement, however, demands a new conception of atonement or reconciliation: a conception revealing not simply that God is the author and the agent of atonement but is himself the subject of reconciliation as well. We have seen that radical faith knows the transcendent epiphany of Spirit as an alien and repressive form of God, and Hegel would teach us that it is only in the modern world or in an absolute form of faith that consciousness can know that transcendent Spirit is abstract and lifeless, for only by means of a realization of the death of God in human experience can faith be liberated from the authority and the power of the primordial God. Once God has died in Christ to his transcendent epiphany, that epiphany must inevitably recede into an abstract and alien form, eventually becoming the full embodiment of every alien other, and thence appearing to consciousness as the ultimate source of all repression. Already we have seen that faith can name this movement as the metamorphosis of God into Satan, as God empties himself of his original power and glory and progressively becomes manifest as an alien but oppressive nothingness. We must understand this whole movement as an atoning process, a forward-moving process wherein a vacuous and nameless power of evil becomes increasingly manifest as the dead body of God or Satan; but it is precisely this epiphany of God as Satan which numbs the power of evil, and unveils every alien and oppressive other as a backward-moving regression into the now lifeless and hence ultimately powerless emptiness of the primordial sacrality of God.

The negation occurring in the Crucifixion therefore is not a simple negation, not a mere annullment or annihilation of a previously existent Being, but rather the negation of a negation, the reversal and transformation of the fallen or transcendent epiphany of Spirit. Yes, God dies in the Crucifixion: therein he fulfills the movement of the Incarnation by totally emptying himself of his primordial sacrality. But his death is a self-negation or self-annihilation: consequently, by freely willing the dissolution of His transcendent "Selfhood," the Godhead reverses the life and movement of the transcendent realm, transforming transcendence into immanence, thereby abolishing the ground of every alien other. If we conceive the Crucifixion as the original enactment and embodiment of the self-reversal of all transcendent life and power, then we can understand the atonement as a universal process, a process present wherever there is life and energy, wherever alienation and repression are abolished by the self-negation of their ultimate source. However, the abolition of alienation and repression must remain illusory if it is not the expression of the self-negation or self-annihilation of God. Alienation and repression must forever rule in history if it is impossible to abolish their ground; so long as the ultimate ground of a fallen history remains wholly isolated and absolutely autonomous, there can be no hope in the resurrection of energy and life. Yet the God who died in Christ has freely annulled the final ground of repression: by annihilating his original epiphany, he has shattered all abstract and alien forms of Spirit, finally bringing an end to the life and movement of a transcendent or wholly other beyond, thereby obliterating the ground of all No-saying, and dissolving every sanction for a regressive movement to immobility and silence.

While it is true that the event of the Crucifixion, or the movement of the universal process of atonement, reveals the self-estrangement of God, a polarity manifesting itself in the yawning chasm between the Father and the Son, a consistent and radical form of faith must never fall into a nondialectical dualism by wholly isolating the alien God and the incarnate Word. Recognizing that the Crucifixion is an act of atonement, an act reversing the primordial sacrality of God, we must not imagine that it is consumed in the emptying of the transcendent sacred, but rather conceive its consummation as the final extension of an emptied and negated sacrality throughout the totality of experience. Not until a self-negated sacrality has entered into the fullness of experience will it fulfill the movement of the atonement. Just as the Crucifixion cannot truly be known as the mere negation of transcendence, it is necessary to understand the atonement as a negative process of reversing every alien other, a process of negating all negations. It, too, is a kenotic process, for it is the embodiment in history and experience of the divine process, and it effects a self-negation or self-annihilation of every power confining life and energy. Even the most awesome and oppressive manifestations of an alien otherness are finally subject to a dialectical reversal, a reversal that has already occurred in the self-annihilation of God, but only with the extension of this reversal into every alien sphere will the actualization of the atonement be consummated. Satan must become totally and comprehensively present in his apocalyptic form as the lifeless residue of the self-negation of God before the atonement will have become wholly actualized in history; and then, the radical apocalyptic seer assures us, Satan must undergo a final metamorphosis into an eschatological epiphany of Christ.

No doubt the total vision promised by an apocalyptic form of faith is not yet present upon our historical horizon; for, immersed as we are in a fully profane consciousness, we would seem to have lost the very possibility of apocalyptic vision. Not until our time did the meaning and the reality of the radical profane become embedded in human consciousness, because ours is the first form of consciousness to have evolved after the historical actualization of the death of God. Nevertheless, the modern artist, by inverting or reversing our mythical traditions, has disclosed a totally immanent mode of existence banished even from the memory of transcendence, and created a comprehensive vision of a new and total nothingness which Blake named as Ulro, or Hell. In 1822, Blake etched *The Ghost of Abel,* "A Revelation in the Visions of Jehovah Seen by William Blake," and the poem on this single plate was destined to be the last prophetic poetry that Blake was to give to the world. After the death of Abel, his ghost appears, demanding vengeance, then sinks into his grave, from which Satan arises, demanding of Jehovah the sacrifice of men, and foreseeing that: "Thou shalt Thyself be Sacrificed to Me, thy God, on Calvary." But Jehovah thunders and replies:

> "Such is My Will that Thou Thyself go to Eternal
> Death
> In Self-Annihilation, even till Satan, Self-subdu'd,
> Put off Satan
> Into the Bottomless Abyss, whose torment arises
> for ever & ever."

Compressed as these lines are, they contain the dual theme that God must be sacrificed to Satan on Calvary, and that

Satan must be self-annihilated and forever perish as Satan. Once again Blake is envisioning a revolutionary transformation of Christianity. Believing that every repression of energy is a repetition of Calvary, Blake finally came to see that the very horror of the sacrifice which Satan demands in all his multiple forms is ultimately a redemptive horror, a darkness which must become light. This is because the movement of the energy of passion is kenotic or sacrificial, both in origin and in goal: therefore an energy becoming actualized or incarnate in the flesh must be self-subdued in self-annihilation. Can this mean that, apocalyptically and dialectically envisioned, Satan is the Christian name of the atoning power and presence of Christ?

In his commentary on *Jerusalem,* Joseph Wicksteed notes—but unfortunately he fails to develop or explicate this insight—that Blake's Christ is the redeemer of the Creator. Christ is the redeemer because he is the full actualization of kenotic energy; but the Creator, or the wholly alien and transcendent epiphany of Spirit, is the redeemed because an absolutely transcendent and sovereign God is finally the source of all that repressed energy which is transmuted in self-sacrifice. Thus the Creator is the spectrous "Shadow" of a fallen and inverted energy, and his shadow disappears in the kenotic passion of self-sacrifice and self-annihilation. "I am not a God afar off," declares the Savior in *Jerusalem,* but in the Lamb's presence the distant God is self-annihilated and forever perishes as Satan: "Thou shalt Thyself be Sacrificed to Me, thy God, on Calvary." So long as Christianity knows the Crucifixion as a vicarious sacrifice for a totally guilty humanity, as the innocent sacrifice of the eternal Son of God to a just but merciful Father, it can never celebrate the definitive victory of the Crucifixion; for such a redeemed humanity remains in bondage to the transcendent Judge, and must continue to be submissive to his distant and alien authority, ever pleading for mercy when it falls away from his absolute command. If the

Crucifixion does not express and embody a decisive self-transformation of God, then at most it can only give a guilty humanity a temporary respite from the sovereign power of the transcendent Creator, while at worst it can seal a fallen humanity in its abject state of powerlessness and self-abasement, totally repressing every tendency to movement and life. The radical Christian, who is in quest of a total redemption, must repudiate every religious promise resting upon a perpetuation of man's fallen state, and recognize in the orthodox image of the crucified Christ an image of the victory of that Satan who would bind man to a broken and shrunken condition. Not until the Christian recognizes the Crucifixion as enacting and embodying the self-negation of the sovereign and transcendent Creator can he celebrate an atonement which is the source of the abolition of all confinement and repression.

Hegel, in those difficult, often cryptic, but nevertheless profoundly rewarding pages in the final sections of *The Phenomenology of Spirit,* where he discusses Christianity as the "absolute religion," gives witness to the advent of an absolute form of Christianity which both negates all previous religion and promises a reconciliation of all those antinomies which have plagued human consciousness throughout its history. While Blake struggled with great difficulty to create a consistent dialectical vision of the atonement as a universal process, Hegel's philosophical method leads to an understanding of the ground of such a vision, and for that very reason the philosopher's ideas can illuminate the dark if deeper vision of the poet. Hegel is all too Blakean in understanding the Crucifixion as the sacrifice of the abstract and alien God. Indeed, Hegel attempts to demonstrate that the Crucifixion can only fully appear and be real in consciousness when God is known as being alienated from himself, existing in a dichotomous form as Father and Son or sovereign Creator and eternal Word. To maintain his existence as the transcendent Creator, God must continually cancel or negate the world; but to move toward his universal epiphany as the Incarnate Word, he must negate his sovereign transcendence. Consequently, God is here known as existing in opposition to himself. The dissolution of this opposition takes place only when each form of the Godhead, by virtue of its inherent independence, dissolves itself in itself: "Therefore that element which has for its essence, not independent self-existence but simple being, is what empties and abandons itself, gives itself unto death, and so reconciles Absolute Being with its own self." Spirit now becomes manifest in its ultimate form, yet it comes to its own fulfillment in the sphere of the immediate and sensuous present, as the dissolution of the alienated forms of the Godhead reconciles that Godhead with the actuality of immediate existence.

Through the events that faith knows as the Incarnation and the Crucifixion, God empties himself of his sovereignty and transcendence, and not only does this kenotic sacrifice effect the dissolution of the opposition between Father and Son in the new epiphany of God as universal Spirit, but so likewise vanishes the opposition between God and the world. As the full meaning of this sacrifice or self-negation dawns in consciousness, the factuality and historicity of Jesus' particular "self-existence" is negated as that existence now becomes universal self-consciousness: "The death of the mediator is death not merely of his *natural* aspect, of his particular self-existence: what dies is not merely the outer casement, which, being stripped of essential being, is *eo ipso* dead, but also the abstraction of the divine Being." Therefore spiritual Christianity, as Hegel conceives it, understands the atoning death of Christ as the manifestation of the transition of Spirit from its alienated epiphany as transcendent Being to its final epiphany as incarnate Spirit, or what Hegel termed "total self-consciousness." This transition is effected by the death of the abstract and alien

God in the kenotic process of Incarnation and Crucifixion; but a religious form of faith can only grasp this process as a series of events that are autonomous and external to human consciousness. Only when the death of God appears in all its bitterness in the "unhappy Consciousness," and consciousness thence comes to know the dissolution of the Wholly Other, can a spiritual form of dialectical understanding arise that will know the death of God as the triumphant epiphany of Spirit. For so long as consciousness remains bound to religion, it must exist in an alienated form, closed to the inner reality of Spirit by its very belief in an alien Other. This traditional form of faith is the product of a divided consciousness: it can only know redemption as a reconciliation with an Other lying beyond itself, and must experience the actuality of the present as a world merely awaiting its transfiguration. Yet Christianity has now at least implicitly evolved to an absolute form wherein it can realize the final epiphany of Spirit as immediately present and actualized for us.

All too obviously, however, our world is not bathed in an epiphany of light. Indeed, the contemporary Christian is confronted with a world of total darkness, a darkness dissolving or negating everything that Christianity once knew as faith. If a new and total Antichrist has appeared upon our horizon, and is destined to become yet more fully incarnate in the world, then we must learn from the apocalyptic and radical Christian to greet his epiphany not only with horror but also with the joy of faith. The fact that artists and seers have succeeded in naming our darkness, in speaking in the presence of the most awesome nothingness yet actualized in history, is a decisive sign of new life and affirmation, a life that can speak and move even in the presence of a life-negating Totality. Like the ancient apocalyptic seer, the modern artist has unveiled a world of darkness, but whereas earlier seers could know a darkness penetrated by a new aeon of light, the contemporary artist has seen light itself as darkness, and embodied in his work an all-embracing vacuity dissolving every previous form of life and light. Nevertheless, the Christian can name an empty and life-negating Totality as the body of the Antichrist. The Christian, moreover, who knows the Christ who is the embodiment of the self-negation of God, can know the Satan or the Antichrist who is present to us as the actualization or the historical realization of the death of God. Insofar as an eschatological epiphany of Christ can occur only in conjunction with a realization in total experience of the kenotic process of self-negation, we should expect that epiphany to occur in the heart of darkness, for only the universal triumph of the Antichrist can provide an arena for the total manifestation of Christ. Thus the Christian must finally rejoice in the advent of a total darkness, because the Christian knows the reign of the Antichrist as the darkness before the dawn, a darkness that must ultimately pass away by being transfigured into light.

The radical Christian repudiates the Christian dogma of the resurrection of Christ and his ascension into a celestial and transcendent realm because radical faith revolves about a participation in the Christ who is fully and totally present to us. Speaking in the traditional symbolic language of Christianity, we could say that radical faith transposes the traditional vision of the resurrection into a contemporary vision of the descent into Hell: the crucified Christ does not ascend to a heavenly realm but rather descends ever more fully into darkness and flesh. By this means we can see that the continuing descent of the Word into flesh clearly parallels the historical actualization of the death of God and God's final appearance in our history in a totally alien and lifeless form. Finally, the dead body of God cannot be dissociated from the Christ who has descended into Hell. We must not imagine that a movement of Word or Spirit into flesh is liberating and redemptive in a simple and nondialectical sense: a metamorphosis of Word into flesh must reverse the original redemptive potency of Spirit and extend that reversal throughout the whole range of experience. As the original form of Spirit progressively recedes into a faceless immobility, that blank and numbing silence becomes manifest throughout experience, abolishing every transcendent ground of hope and stilling every nostalgic aspiration for a garden of innocence. Once the transcendent realm has lost every sign of its original redemptive power, then it must become manifest as a negative or demonic transcendence, before its passage into total formlessness. It is not without significance that the modern artist has given himself so fully to envisioning evil and nothingness, or has been so deeply bound to visions of Satan, of chaos, and of emptiness; for the artist cannot escape the reality of his time by fleeing to an earlier moment of history. A new epiphany of Antichrist is drawing everything into itself, as its ever dawning totality transfigures all experience, unveiling the emptiness of Hell in every human hand and face.

Yet if the Christian can but name our Hell as Antichrist, then we shall know that its power has been broken and it can pose no ultimate threat to us. When all evil and nothingness pass into the faceless epiphany of a total Antichrist, then the ultimate ground of chaos will be dissolved, every inherent sanction for all alien and compelling demands will be removed, and every opposing other will stand revealed in a lifeless and vacuous form. The reign of the Antichrist is the consummation of all oppressive power because it embodies every alien other in its pure and intrinsic otherness, dissolving once and for all the deceptive mask of evil, and actualizing an underlying and hidden chaos in the fullness of a now naked experience. It is precisely because an epiphany of Antichrist abolishes the transcendent source of evil and nothingness by embodying a primordial chaos in the actuality of history that it is a redemptive epiphany, an epiphany unveiling the full reality of alienation and repression, thereby preparing the way for their ultimate reversal. Therefore the Christian is finally called to accept the Antichrist, or the totality of the dead body of God, as a final kenotic manifestation of Christ. Distant as we ourselves may actually be from such an apocalyptic vision, a vision that is already clearly present in Blake, we must nevertheless be prepared to open ourselves to the anguish and terror of experience as an expression of the atoning process of redemption, a process that even now is unveiling a yet fuller form of horror by dissolving the sacred and transcendent masks of experience, and actualizing experience in a totally immanent form. Perhaps we cannot yet name such an experience as the atoning body of Christ; but we can know it as the dead and alien body of God, and consequently we cannot dissociate the alien body of the Antichrist from the Christ who is the embodiment of the self-negation of God.

III. THE FORGIVENESS OF SIN

Protestant dialectical theologians from Luther to Barth have insisted that we only truly know our fallen and sinful condition as a consequence of the gift of grace, that only a realization of redemption or of the forgiveness of sin makes possible an understanding of the reality of sin. Nevertheless, Christian theology has almost entirely reached its conception of sin either from the postulation of a natural and universal moral law or from the situation of a broken and guilty humanity confronting an absolutely sovereign Creator and Judge. When theology draws its conception of sin either from a normative understanding of law or an analysis of the state of the sinner, it isolates sin from grace, and thus forecloses the possibility of understanding the forgiveness or the annulment of sin. Perhaps the Old Testament words most clearly preparing the way for the Christian proclamation of the forgiveness of sin are contained in a postexilic prophecy recorded in The Book of Jeremiah, a joyous prophecy embodying the initial promise of a new covenant:

> Behold, the days are coming, says the Lord, when I will make a new covenant with the house of Israel and the house of Judah, not like the covenant which I made with their fathers when I took them by the hand to bring them out of the land of Egypt, my covenant which they broke, though I was their husband, says the Lord. But this is the covenant which I will make with the house of Israel after those days, says the Lord: I will put my law within them, and I will write it upon their hearts; and I will be their God, and they shall be my people. And no longer shall each man teach his neighbor and each his brother, saying, "Know the Lord," for they shall all know me, from the least of them to the greatest, says the Lord; for I will forgive their iniquity, and I will remember their sin no more. (Jer. 31:31-34.)

It is the final phrase of this prophecy which supplies a crucial key to the radical Christian vision: "I will remember their sin no more." Remarkably enough, these words have no clear analogue in the New Testament, but the radical Christian joins the greatest reformers of the Christian faith in discovering that the forgiveness of sin culminates in an abolition of the memory of sin.

If we know anything at all about the ministry of Jesus, we know that no action of his ministry brought greater offense to his hearer than his forgiveness of sin; and no theme of his sayings or parables overshadows the proclamation of forgiveness, although we must recognize that originally this forgiveness was inseparable from the eschatological situation of the dawning of the Kingdom of God. We can sense something of the early Christian understanding of the eschatological meaning of the new covenant by noting the words of Paul, who, while speaking of the old covenant as a law of death and condemnation, rejoices that the glory of the new covenant so surpasses the glory of the old that the old covenant now has no glory at all:

> Since we have such a hope, we are very bold, not like Moses, who put a veil over his face so that the Israelites might not see the end of the fading splendor. But their minds were hardened; for to this day, when they read the old covenant, that same veil remains unlifted, because only through Christ is it taken away. Yes, to this day whenever Moses is read a veil lies over their minds; but when a man turns to the Lord the veil is removed. Now the Lord is the Spirit, and where the Spirit of the Lord is, there is freedom. And we all, with unveiled face, beholding the glory of the Lord, are being changed into his likeness from one degree of glory to another; for this comes from the Lord who is the Spirit. (II Cor. 3:12-18.)

A radical Christian would interpret these words as meaning that the glory of the God of the old covenant is abolished, for apart from an abolition of the God of judgment, there remains no possibility of transforming humanity into the likeness or image of the glory of Christ. Accordingly, radical or spiritual Christians believe that the demands of the God of law and judgment are annulled in the grace of the God who died on Calvary. Yet this grace cannot be realized or fulfilled until it culminates in the cessation of the very memory of sin: indeed, Kierkegaard underwent his second conversion or "metamorphosis" only when he finally came to realize that God had *forgotten* his sin, and then wrote *The Sickness Unto Death,* whose dialectical thesis is that sin is the opposite not of virtue but of faith.

When faith understands itself as existing in opposition to the state of sin, it must give itself both to a negation of law and guilt and to a continual process of abolishing the consciousness of sin: "Come, O thou Lamb of God, and take away the remembrance of Sin" (*Jerusalem* 50:24). Seen in this perspective, guilt is the product of self-alienation: and not simply an alienation from an individual and private selfhood, but rather a cosmic state of alienation from a universal energy and life.

> In Great Eternity every particular Form gives
>   forth or Emanates
> Its own peculiar Light, & the Form is the Divine
>   Vision
> And the Light is his Garment. This is Jerusalem
>   in every Man,
> A Tent & Tabernacle of Mutual Forgiveness, Male
>   & Female Clothings.
> And Jerusalem is called Liberty among the Chil-
>   dren of Albion.

Although Jerusalem is present in every "Man" as a tabernacle of mutual forgiveness, that tabernacle has been shattered by the Fall, as fallen man is sealed in the isolation of his individual selfhood:

> But Albion fell down, a Rocky fragment from
>   Eternity hurl'd
> By his own Spectre, who is the Reasoning Power
>   in every Man,
> Into his own Chaos, which is the Memory between
>   Man & Man.
>   (*Jerusalem* 54:1-8.)

To name chaos as the memory separating man from man is to recognize that sin is a state of solitude, with the consequence that the forgiveness of sin is a cosmic process of "Self-Annihilation." Furthermore, the forgiveness of sin is a universal and apocalyptic process of redemption: all those spaces separating a fallen humanity from its isolated parts must be annulled by a forward-moving process drawing the apocalyptic futurity of Jerusalem into the present moment, thereby making possible the final triumph of "The Great Humanity Divine."

Blake's most luminous vision of "Self-Annihilation" is contained in the second book of *Milton,* where Milton or a reborn Christianity undergoes regeneration by transforming Satan into "The Great Humanity Divine." This vision

of the mature Blake is accompanied by a new conception
of the relation between human individuals and their chang-
ing states:

> Distinguish therefore States from Individuals in
> those States.
> States Change, but Individual Identities never
> change nor cease.
> You cannot go to Eternal Death in that which can
> never Die.
>
> (*Milton* 32:22-24.)

While individual identities never die, all that which they
become in history and experience must pass through an
eternal death, and it is precisely this passage through death
which effects a cosmic and total regeneration. Milton, the
human state called "Eternal Annihilation," has, in his own
state of self-negation, the power to annihilate that Satan
who appears within the deadly "Selfhood." But following
the "Laws of Eternity," he annihilates himself for Satan's
good: "Such are the Laws of Eternity, that each shall mu-
tually/Annihilate himself for others' good, as I for thee"
(38:35). Repudiating the fear and dread inspired in men
by Satan and his churches—an *Angst* deriving from an
abject and selfish terror of death (38:38)—Milton's purpose is to teach men to despise death and to move forward:

> "In fearless majesty annihilating Self, laughing to
> scorn
> Thy Laws & terrors, shaking down thy Synagogues
> as webs.
> I come to discover before Heav'n & Hell the Self
> righteousness
> In all its Hypocritic turpitude, opening to every
> eye
> These wonders of Satan's holiness, shewing to the
> Earth
> The Idol Virtues of the Natural Heart, & Satan's
> Seat
> Explore in all its Selfish Natural Virtue . . . "
>
> (*Milton* 38:41-47.)

We must not fail to observe, however, that here God is revealed in his satanic form only in response to a humanity that has passed through "Self-Annihilation" and abolished even the memory of sin. It is only when man has been delivered from the threat of condemnation, a threat always present wherever humanity exists in a state of isolated selfhood, that a truly forgiven humanity can be liberated from Satan's power.

When self-righteousness and natural virtue are unveiled as Satan's holiness, we are once again confronting a transcendence and inversion of the Western moral and theological tradition, an inversion revealing that the natural virtue and power of an individual selfhood is the inevitable expression of the self-alienation of a fallen and isolated humanity. Moreover, so long as self-righteousness is judged to be a moral state deriving from an isolated and autonomous individual, there lies no way to a comprehension of its ultimate ground and its universal consequences. The regenerate Milton moves through a self-annihilation actualizing the death of God in immediate experience. Thereby the living power of the transcendent and omnipotent Judge is transposed in human experience into the dead body of Satan, as Milton's passage through the death of selfhood unveils the ground of an isolated selfhood as that chasm separating the creature from the Creator, thus making possible the reversal or dissolution of natural virtue and self-righteousness in the immediate and present actualization of the self-annihilation of God. Once God has ceased to exist in human experience as the omnipotent and numinous Lord, there perishes with him every moral imperative addressed to man from a beyond, and humanity ceases to be imprisoned by an obedience to an external will or authority. In *The Everlasting Gospel,* Blake presents a simple but powerful evocation of this antinomian theme, as can be seen in these lines recounting Jesus' reaction to the woman taken in adultery (who is blasphemously identified with Mary, the mother of Jesus):

What was the sound of Jesus' breath?
He laid His hand on Moses' Law:
The Ancient Heavens, in Silent Awe
Writ with Curses from Pole to Pole,
All away began to roll:
The Earth trembling & Naked lay
In secret bed of Mortal Clay,
On Sinai felt the hand divine
Putting back the bloody shrine,
And she heard the breath of God
As she heard by Eden's flood:
"Good & Evil are no more!
Sinai's trumpets, cease to roar!
Cease, finger of God, to write!
The Heavens are not clean in thy Sight.
Thou art Good, & thou Alone;
Nor may the sinner cast one stone.
To be Good only, is to be
A God or else a Pharisee."

(2e, 10-28.)

Good and evil cease to be when man is delivered from self-hood, when his solitary and autonomous ego is abolished, and he ceases to be aware of a distance separating himself from others. That very distance is solidified by the demands of a distant Lord, and apart from a fallen confinement in an isolated selfhood there could be no awareness of the God who is the Wholly Other.

If a universal and fallen condition of selfhood isolates man from man and man from God, then sin is equivalent to this cosmic state of isolation, and the forgiveness of sin must be a cosmic and historical process that negates this estrangement by annihilating the solitude that is its source. On the 96th plate of *Jerusalem,* there is an illustration of the Creator and Jerusalem drawing together in an ecstatic embrace. The Creator is on the left and is moving downward toward Jerusalem in his final manifestation as Satan, while Jerusalem, or the apocalyptic epiphany of Christ, appears as a naked female form moving upward toward Satan. Satan ("The Ancient of Days") looks to the right and exposes his right foot from beneath his covering veil, both of which symbolize a spiritual ascent; whereas, Jerusalem, who unlike her divine counterpart is facing us, rises on her left foot and looks to her right and our left, as she ascends by descending, by reversing the divine movement ("the way up is the way down"). We may surmise that this illustration is a vision of the universal process of atonement if only because Satan and Jerusalem are engaged in a mutual negation of all that selfhood isolating each from the other: Satan reverses his transcendent selfhood so as to become "flesh" (i.e., *sarx,* in the Pauline sense of existence outside of or apart from Spirit), and Jerusalem completes her reverse movement of ascent by descending into Hell. The text on this plate is saturated with apocalyptic imagery; it opens with a vision of the sun and moon leading forward the "Vision of Heaven & Earth," which is immediately followed by an apocalyptic epiphany of Jesus as the Son of Man: "And the Divine Appearance was the likeness & similitude of Los." However, the traditional apocalyptic symbol of the Son of Man is a symbol of a heavenly and divine Being; and his epiphany—which marks the advent of the final Eschaton—occurs in the heavens, where he appears with legions of angels. Blake dialectically inverts this ancient symbol so as to transpose it into the kenotic Christ: hence Jesus appears in the likeness of Los or the temporal form of the "Human Imagination."

We must not dissociate the lines of the text from their accompanying illustration, for the apocalyptic epiphany of Jesus occurs when Satan and Jerusalem engage in a mutual embrace. This ecstatic union of Satan and Jerusalem is in process of fulfillment even as Albion (Blake's symbolic figure representing a universal but fallen humanity) experiences the final epiphany of Jesus. The Satan of the illustration has his back turned toward us, and in the lines directly facing his awesome buttocks, Albion laments his cruel and deceitful "Selfhood," recognizing that the God of Sinai has

ensnared him in a deadly sleep of six thousand years: "I
know it is my Self, O my Divine Creator & Redeemer."
These words are addressed to Jesus, and we must not fail
to notice that the transcendent Creator and Judge can be
identified as the ultimate ground of selfhood only at the
moment when an immanent and totally human Jesus can
be named as the divine Creator and Redeemer! Nothing
less is occurring here than an apocalyptic *coincidentia oppositorum,* and while such a radical dialectical inversion
has never previously occurred in the apocalyptic tradition,
when it occurs in this initial form it is accompanied by a
vision of a total process of redemption that is effected by a
divine passage through death. Thus Jesus responds to Albion's terror of his own selfhood with these words: "Fear
not Albion: unless I die thou canst not live;/But if I die
I shall arise again & thou with me. . . ."

> So Jesus spoke: the Covering Cherub coming on
> in darkness
> Overshadow'd them, & Jesus said: "Thus do Men
> in Eternity
> One for another to put off, by forgiveness, every
> sin."

The Satan whose darkness engulfs both Jerusalem and
Jesus and Albion is the Satan who finally undergoes a total
reversal by dying in Jesus' death:

> Jesus said: "Wouldest thou love one who never
> died
> For thee, or ever die for one who had not died for
> thee?
> And if God dieth not for Man & giveth not him-
> self
> Eternally for Man, Man could not exist; for Man
> is Love
> As God is Love: every kindness to another is a
> little Death
> In the Divine Image, nor can Man exist but by
> Brotherhood."

While Satan's embrace of Jerusalem can only be consummated in death, that death is a final realization in experience of the self-annihilation of God, thereby effecting the forgiveness of sin by the reversal of all solitary selfhood. The "Divine Image" dies in Jesus and Jerusalem so as to abolish the transcendent source of guilt and judgment and bring about an apocalyptic and total union of God and man, a union abolishing both transcendence and selfhood, and actualizing a new Totality of "Love." Consequently, the forgiveness of sin is an atoning process embodying the progressive realization in experience of the self-annihilation of God, and it must culminate in an apocalyptic epiphany of "The Great Humanity Divine."

V

A Wager

I. THE LIVING CHRIST

FROM THE point of view of radical Christianity, the original heresy was the identification of the Church as the body of Christ. When the Church is known as the body of Christ, and the Church is further conceived as a distinct and particular institution or organism existing within but nevertheless apart from the world, then the body of Christ must inevitably be distinguished from and even opposed to the body of humanity. Only a religious form of Christianity could establish such a chasm between Christ and the world: for it is the backward movement of religious Christianity which retreats from the world, regressing to a primordial deity which it dares to name as the cosmic Logos and the monarchic Christ. We must not be misled by the emergence of Catholic Christianity into thinking that an increasingly universal form of the Church gives witness to a genuinely forward movement of the Church. A forward movement evolving by means of an extension and enlargement of its given or original form cannot evolve to a truly new and comprehensive universality, nor can it embody the kenotic process of the Incarnation. Thus a forward movement in this sense is finally the expression of the will to power, an all too human regression to an inhuman or prehuman state, which necessarily entails a reversal of the true humanity of Jesus. Once the Church had claimed to be the body of Christ, it had already set upon the imperialistic path of conquering the world, of bringing the life and movement of the world into submission to the inhuman authority and power of an infinitely distant Creator and Judge.

But by identifying the Church's Christ as a reversal of the incarnate Christ, a reversal effected by a backward movement to the now emptied preincarnate epiphanies of God, the radical Christian points the way to the presence of the living Christ in the actuality and fullness of history. It is precisely because the orthodox image of Christ is an image of lordship and power that it is a reversal of a kenotic Christ. The mere fact that the Christ of Christian orthodoxy is an exalted and transcendent Lord is a sufficient sign to the radical Christian that Christianity has reversed the movement of the Incarnation. Simply by clinging to the religious image of transcendent power, the Church has resisted the self-negating movement of Christ and foreclosed the possibility of its own witness to the forward movement of the divine process. Consequently, the radical Christian maintains that it is the Church's regressive religious belief in God which impels it to betray the present and the kenotic reality of Christ. So long as the Church is grounded in the worship of a sovereign and transcendent Lord, and submits in its life and witness to that infinite distance separating the creature and the Creator, it must continue to reverse the movement of the Spirit who progressively becomes actualized as flesh, thereby silencing the life and speech of the Incarnate Word.

Only by recognizing the antithetical relationship that radical faith posits between the primordial and transcendent reality of God and the kenotic and immediate reality of Christ, can we understand the violent attack which the radical Christian launches upon the Christian God. Even the remembrance of the original glory and majesty of God roots the Christian in the past, inducing him to evade the self-emptying negativity of a fully incarnate divine process, and to flee from the Christ who is actual and real in our present. A faith that names Jesus either as the Son of God or as the prophet of God must be a backward movement to a disincarnate and primordial form of Spirit, a movement annulling the events of the Incarnation and the Crucifixion by resurrecting Jesus either in the form of the exalted Lord or as the proclaimer of an already distant and alien majesty of God: hence an orthodox and priestly Christianity is inevitably grounded in the sacred authority and power of the past. How can the Christian know the living Christ who is immediately present to us, a Christ who is the consequence of the continual forward movement and self-negation of the divine process, if he is bound to a long-distant epiphany of Christ which has been emptied and left behind by the progressive movement of the Word's becoming flesh? A Christ appearing to our consciousness in his ancient and traditional form cannot be the true and the living Christ, unless we are to deny the real and forward movement of the Incarnation. Above all, a Christ who even now is manifest in the preincarnate form and epiphany of God, and who can be reached only by a total reversal of our history and experience, must be named as the Antichrist, as the dead and alien body of the God who originally died in Christ. Thus it is the radical Christian proclamation of the death of God which liberates the Christian from every alien and lifeless image of Christ.

Radical Christianity poses the real question which must now be addressed to the Christian: is faith speakable or livable in the actuality of our present? Already we have seen that Christianity is the only form of faith which is not grounded in a backward movement of involution and return. Accordingly, authentic Christianity must move forward through history and experience to an eschatological goal. If Christianity refuses the destiny before it, renouncing the actuality of the time and space which it confronts, then inevitably it must regress to a pre-Christian or non-Christian form. Now we must not confuse a Christian and eschatological passage through the actuality of history and experience with a mere submission to the brute reality of the world; such a submission does not affect the world, nor does it embody a self-negation or self-annihilation of the Incarnate Word. We must, rather, understand the forward movement of Christianity to be a truly negative or self-emptying process, a process simultaneously negating both the Word and world which it embodies, and therefore a process transcending and moving beyond the initial expressions of its own movement. Such a process can be actual and real only by occurring in the actuality of experience; it must move through diverse and ever fuller forms of experience to new and progressively more universal goals. A faith reflecting and witnessing to this process obviously cannot retain a static and unchanging form; instead, it must undergo a continual metamorphosis, a progressive metamorphosis embodying the gradual but continual descent of the Word into flesh. Faith must always be able to speak of the Word which is actually present, and to speak to the actuality of the world and experience which it confronts; otherwise, it will relapse into immobility and silence, thereby betraying the very vocation of faith. Perhaps the religious Christian can believe that Christianity need not know the Christ who is immediately present; but a Christianity divorced from the living presence and action of Christ is a Christianity that has abandoned the specifically Christian movement of faith.

Can we truly speak of the Christ who is present to us, of the living Christ who is actually manifest in our world, and who even now is making all things new? We are forewarned that a contemporary Christ will by no means be identical with the Christ of our Christian past, except insofar as he too is a kenotic Christ who is moving ever more comprehensively into the depths of life and experience. By following the way of the radical Christian, we can rejoice in the death of God, and be assured that the historical realization of the death of God is a full unfolding of the forward movement of the Incarnation. Just as the Crucifixion embodies and makes finally real a divine movement from transcendence to immanence, a movement of an originally transcendent God into the actuality of life and experience, so too the dawning of the death of God throughout the totality of experience progressively annuls every human or actual possibility of returning to transcendence. It is precisely because the movement of the Incarnation has now become manifest in every human hand and face, dissolving even the memory of God's original transcendent life and redemptive power, that there can no longer be either a truly contemporary movement to transcendence or an active and living faith in the transcendent God.

Only by accepting and even willing the death of God in our experience can we be liberated from a transcendent beyond, an alien beyond which has been emptied and darkened by God's self-annihilation in Christ. To the extent that we attempt to cling to a transcendent realm, a realm that has become ever darker and emptier in the actuality of our experience, we must be closed to the actual presence of the living Christ, and alienated from the contemporary movement of the divine process. Every death of a divine image is a realization of the kenotic movement, an actualization in consciousness and experience of God's death in Christ; thus a fully incarnate Christ will have dissolved or reversed all sacred images by the very finality of his movement into flesh. We know the finality of the Incarnation by knowing that God is dead; and once we fully live the death of God, we will be liberated from the temptation to return to an epiphany of deity which is present only in the past. Yet to recognize the Christ who has become manifest and real as the result of a total movement from transcendence to immanence, we must be freed from every attachment to transcendence, and detached from all yearning for a primordial innocence. A truly contemporary Christ cannot become present to us until we ourselves have died to every shadow and fragment of his transcendent image.

We must not deceive ourselves by thinking that the faith and worship of the Church must inevitably give witness to a contemporary epiphany of Christ. No doubt, the Incarnate Word is never without witness, but we have little reason to believe that a Christ who has fully and totally entered the world could be known by a Church that refuses either to abandon its transcendent image of Christ or to negate its religious movement of involution and return. If Christ is truly present and real to us in a wholly incarnate epiphany, then the one principle that can direct our search for his presence is the negative principle that he can no longer be clearly or decisively manifest in any of his previous forms or images. All established Christian authority has now been shattered and broken: the Bible may well embody a revelation of the Word but we have long since lost any certain or even clear means of interpreting its meaning as revelation; the Church in its liturgies, creeds, and confessions may well embody an epiphany of Christ, but that epiphany is distant from us, and it cannot speak to our contemporary experience. Even the language that the Christian once employed in speaking of Christ has become archaic and empty, and we could search in vain for a traditional Christian language and symbolism in contemporary art and thinking.

If we are honestly to embark upon a quest for a truly contemporary epiphany of Christ, we must be prepared to accept an ultimate risk, a genuine risk dissolving all certainty and security whatsoever. Let us note, however, that authentic faith always entails a risk of a high order, and this risk must vary in accordance with the time and situation in which it occurs. Already the modern traditional or orthodox Christian has made a wager incorporating such a risk: he has bet that Jesus Christ is the same yesterday, today, and forever, and thus he has bet that finally there is only a single image or epiphany of Jesus, regardless of the time or history in which it appears. The modern dimension of this wager is that our time is so obviously divorced from the time of Jesus, or, at least, our world and history is clearly estranged from the classical world of Christendom,

with the consequence that to choose the traditional form
of Christ is either to set oneself against the contemporary
world or to decide that the actuality of one's time and situation can have no bearing upon one's faith in Christ. Never
before has this consequence become so clearly manifest,
because, as we previously observed, ours is the first form
of consciousness and experience that has evolved after the
full historical realization of the death of God. This means
that any contemporary wager upon the Christ of Christian
orthodoxy must be willing to forfeit all the life and movement of a world and actuality that has negated or dissolved
the Christian God. We cannot pretend that an ultimate
faith in the transcendent Christ of the Church can have no
effect upon the actuality of the believer's life in the world,
nor can we imagine that the Church can change its language about Christ in accordance with the actual world
which it confronts without in any way decisively effecting
its faith in Christ. No, the fact remains that the Christian today who chooses the orthodox image of Christ is
making a wager in which he stands to forfeit all the life
and energy of a world that is totally alien to the Church's
Christ.

Of course, few Christians are consciously or fully aware
that they must make such a choice. But true faith is impossible apart from a risk, and the Christian who now
chooses the traditional form of Christ is risking not only
the loss of the actuality of the present but also the loss of
the Christ who may be fully incarnate in that present. Now
we must pose a contrary wager. Dare we bet upon a totally
incarnate Christ, whose contemporary presence negates
his previous epiphanies, with the full realization that we are
therein risking both the total loss of Christ as well as the
loss of all that life and energy deriving from the presence
of a transcendent and eternally given Christ? We must be
fully aware that a wager upon a totally incarnate Christ is
every bit as much a wager as a wager upon the orthodox
image of Christ. Either risks losing both the true reality of

Christ and all that life evolving from the presence of Christ. Both are genuine expressions of faith because each enacts a genuine wager, and they are united in repudiating any form of faith that does not demand an ultimate wager. The radical Christian who chooses a fully contemporary Christ not only must be willing to abandon the Christ of our Christian past but he must accept the fact that no clear path lies present to the Christ whom he has chosen, and no final authority exists to direct him upon his quest. Moreover, the Christian who wagers upon a totally incarnate Christ must negate every form and image of transcendence, regardless of what area of consciousness or experience in which it may appear. Thus he must forswear every transcendent ground of judgment, and be banished from every hope in a transcendent life or power. He has chosen a darkness issuing from the death of every image and symbol of transcendence, and he must bet that the darkness of his destiny is the present form and actuality of a totally incarnate body of Christ.

II. Guilt and Resentment

Nietzsche, the greatest modern master of understanding man, has taught us an ironical and intimately human mode of listening, and this listening is often most effective when it listens to what is not said. The modern Christian, at least to judge by the theological spokesmen of the churches, has very nearly ceased speaking about damnation and Hell, and seemingly is no longer capable of even speaking about an ultimate and final form of guilt. Irony besets every action of that strange creature man, and we can only wonder that the ecclesiastical Christian should have ceased to speak about damnation in a century in which guilt and damnation have become an overwhelming motif in so many of the most creative expressions of consciousness and experience. Is ours not a time in which Hell appears to be the arena of human existence? Yet our theologians no longer speak of

Hell, and great masses of Christians seem to have lost all fear of damnation. While we need not doubt that most ecclesiastical Christians practice Christianity as a heaven-sent way of returning to innocence, why is it that even the wisest and most worldly of our theologians are mute on the subject of damnation? Why can the theologian not speak of Hell, whereas the artist and the thinker often seem to speak of nothing else? Is it the modern religious Christian's inability to speak about a God who is actually present in the world which is the ground of his refusal to share a uniquely modern sense of guilt?

Naïve Christians frequently say that damnation and Hell are Old Testament themes which find no place in the "good news" of the New Testament. But the simple truth is that Hell, Satan, and final damnation are almost uniquely New Testament motifs, and these motifs of ultimate terror play a far greater role in the doctrines and liturgies of Christianity than they do in any other religion. Who else but the Christian fears a final and total damnation? Where else but in Christendom do we find records of an experience of total terror? However, in the modern world we find the strange phenomenon of the Christian who is liberated from the fear of damnation, a Christian who apparently is incapable of experiencing terror. Is this the sign of a mature faith which has finally come of age? Or is it but another sign of the truth of Kierkegaard's judgment that the Christianity of the New Testament no longer exists? Why should the contemporary Christian be innocent of the knowledge of Hell unless the Church has succeeded in establishing itself as a haven from the horror of the modern world? Or is the modern religious Christian so numb with guilt that he can no longer name his condition, and must relapse into a state of immobility and silence about guilt if only as a means of existing in its presence? Is it because the Church can no longer speak about Hell and damnation that we hear so much foolish ecclesiastical chatter about forgiveness? What can an ultimate forgiveness mean if it is impossible to speak about an ultimate guilt? When the Church speaks about guilt, can it be no more than the custodian of the law, ever sanctioning the common fears of society and incorporating in its body whatever is left of the restraints and inhibitions of the society of the past? Is the real function of an all too modern ecclesiastical Christianity to actualize whatever faith and hope is possible for all those masses of men who refuse the darkness and terror of our time?

Nietzsche teaches us that we cannot dissociate the phenomenon of guilt from the phenomenon of pain: it is those who suffer most deeply who are most conscious of guilt, and those who suffer the least who are free of a bad conscience. Of course, suffering in this sense is not to be identified with mere physical pain, but instead is the creation of a full and active consciousness. Nevertheless, a guilty conscience cannot naïvely be judged to be a product of illusion, or of an overly active consciousness, or of simple fear. Guilt is always the consequence of a retreat from life, of a reversal of the life and energy of the body, a reversal having its origin in that repression which is Nietzsche's name for the real ruler of a fallen history. Nietzsche joins Kierkegaard in identifying existence as guilt. For everything that we know as consciousness and experience is grounded in repression, and to broaden or deepen our consciousness is to recognize the power of repression, a power creating all those dualistic oppositions or antinomies which split human existence asunder, dividing and isolating the shrunken energy of life. Accordingly, guilt is a conscious realization of the broken or fallen condition of humanity, and it is actualized in the individual insofar as he becomes consciously aware of his own bondage to repression. But humanity, as the poets tell us, cannot bear much reality; and we escape the pain of our condition by resentment, a resentment attempting to reverse or even to leap out of the actuality of existence. Resentment arises from an inability or refusal to accept the brute reality of the world; it is a rebellion against life itself, a hatred of the pain, the joy, the fullness of existence. Thus, resentment shrinks existence into the narrowest possible bounds, negating every outlet for the release of energy, and condemning every source of movement and life. The great No-sayers are those who have suffered most profoundly, and they have succeeded in creating patterns of resentment which a weak and broken humanity can accept as the way to the dissolution of consciousness and pain.

Yes, we are guilty; or, our given or actual condition is a condition of guilt; but we harden and freeze our guilty condition by a resentment which forecloses the possibility of the abolition of repression. Resentment is a withdrawal from the possibility of life and movement, a negative reaction to the painfulness of the human condition whereby we submit to guilt and alienation by condemning every possibility of accepting and affirming life. Such a submission to guilt is at bottom a submission to pain, or, rather, an attempt to lower the consciousness of pain by shrinking and confining the energy of life. Ultimately, resentment is directed against the cause of pain; and it arises when we become conscious of our painful condition, and attempt to numb our suffering by negating or evading all occasions for pain. Nietzsche commonly associated resentment with the weak, with those who have been defeated and broken by life, and who then negate every challenge to their own submission and withdrawal. Of course, he also teaches us that resentment can express itself in envy, which is itself the expression of an inability to accept the actuality of a given and particular situation. Always, however, resentment is a flight from life, an evasion of the human condition, an assault upon all life and movement as the way to the dissolution of pain. Resentment progressively lowers the threshold of consciousness, reducing experience to ever narrower spheres, or freezing a given state of consciousness by binding it to a hatred of its immediate ground. Thus, resentment must finally sanction the reality of guilt, passively submitting to the brokenness of the human condition, and ruthlessly refusing every promise of forgiveness and life.

A guilty humanity is inevitably conscious of an opposing other, an imperative appearing whenever we become aware of our confinement by recognizing the repressed state of our own energy. The law, Paul teaches, makes us conscious of sin; but we might reverse Paul's dictum and also say that sin and guilt make us conscious of the law. As Augustine so wisely teaches, the deepest attraction of sin is the attraction of the forbidden. The temptation to do the forbidden becomes present only when we become conscious of our own state of repression, and then our attraction to the forbidden deepens our bondage to the law, submitting us ever more fully to its distant and inhuman power. Consequently, repression and guilt are inseparable, or, at least, we become conscious of our guilt only to the extent that we become aware of the power of repression within us. Thence our guilt demands that we be punished, and we indulge in orgies of self-hatred if only as a means of appeasing our bad conscience, a bad conscience which is itself the product of a consciousness of repression. A repressed humanity is a guilty humanity, whether it is conscious of its guilt or not, and to the extent that it becomes conscious of its guilt it must submit to the alien authority of the imperative, an authority sealing the finality of guilt, and binding humanity to perpetual repression. Already in the proclamation of Jesus, however, and in the New Testament messages of Paul and John, we discover the Christian promise of the forgiveness of sin, or the release of the sinner from his bondage to law and judgment, a liberation effected by his participation in the body of Christ or the dawning Kingdom of God. Paul insists that the reign of the law extends throughout the body of a fallen humanity, but it is confined to all that human sphere which does not yet exist in faith, for insofar as we exist in faith we are delivered from the bondage of the law. Indeed, it is only by the gift of freedom in Christ that we become aware of the terrible burden of the law, and only by faith in Christ do we receive the power to name the darkness of sin and guilt. It is by faith alone that we become aware of the true meaning and the overwhelming power of guilt and repression: thus we need have little hesitation in assigning Nietzsche to a tradition of a radical Christian understanding of sin, a tradition going back to Paul by way of Dostoevsky, Kierkegaard, Pascal, Luther, and Augustine.

Moreover, it is of vital importance to realize that while existing in a state of alienation and guilt we ourselves must oppose the other, imposing upon all others the obligation under which we live. When Jesus said, "Judge not," he was calling for an end of all moral judgment, a judgment that must inevitably arise from a condition of guilt. Judgment and forgiveness are poles of an opposing continuum; we judge to the extent that we exist in sin, and we become incapable of judgment to the extent that we are forgiven. The Christian is liberated from the alien power of the moral imperative by virtue of his life in Christ, and faith itself calls upon us to acknowledge that we can be aware of a moral demand only insofar as we are estranged from Christ, and thereby closed to the reality of forgiveness. A guilty humanity can exist only by way of judgment and resentment, a judgment sanctioning its own state of alienation, and a resentment opposing every call to forgiveness. In this perspective we can see that resentment is a flight from the presence of Christ, an opposition to his promise of forgiveness. All too naturally a religious Christianity has known the most awesome and terrifying form of the divine Creator and Judge, for a religious reversal of the Incarnation must resurrect the deity in the form of an absolutely majestic and sovereign power, a power that has now lost its ground in the kenotic movement of the divine process. Thus, too, Christendom has known the most terrible guilt in history, and as a religious Christianity has progressively and ever more fully reversed the movement of the Incarnation, the Christian God has increasingly become alien and abstract, until in our own time he has only been present and real in actual experience in a totally alien form, and the whole body of Western humanity has been initiated into a radical and total state of guilt.

Once again we are called upon to make a wager. Dare we bet that the Christian God is dead, that the ultimate ground of guilt and resentment is broken, and that our guilty condition is created by our clinging to the wholly alien power of a now emptied transcendent realm? If we can truly know that God is dead, and can fully actualize the death of God in our own experience, then we can be liberated from the threat of condemnation, and freed from every terror of a transcendent beyond. Even though we may be mute and speechless in confronting the terror of our time, we cannot evade its pervasive presence, and to relapse into immobility and silence is to foreclose the possibility of being freed from its life-negating power.

Yet the "good news" of the death of God can liberate us from our dread of an alien beyond, releasing us from all attachment to an opposing other, and freeing us for a total participation in the actuality of the immediate moment. By wagering that God is dead, we bet that the awesome and alien power of an infinitely distant and wholly other is finally created by our own guilt and resentment, by our refusal of the life and energy about and within us. Of course, every man who negates and opposes life becomes bound to an alien power. But the Christian knows that Christ is the source of energy and life: hence the Christian must identify all No-saying as a refusal and resistance of Christ. When the Christian bets that God is dead, he is betting upon the real and actual presence of the fully incarnate Christ. Thus a Christian wager upon the death of God is a wager upon the presence of the living Christ, a bet that Christ is now at least potentially present in a new and total form. No, we are not guilty, says the Christian who bets that God is dead. His very bet denies the alien authority of the imperative, and refuses all that guilt arising from a submission to repression. He bets that he is even now forgiven, that he has been delivered from all bondage to the law, and that guilt is finally a refusal of the gift of life and freedom in Christ.

Needless to say, such a wager entails a risk, and an ultimate risk at that. For the Christian who bets that God is dead risks both moral chaos and his own damnation. While the religious or the ecclesiastical Christian has increasingly become incapable of speaking about damnation, the radical Christian, who has been willing to confront the totally alien form of God which has been manifest in our time, has known the horror of Satan and Hell, and can all too readily speak the language of guilt and damnation. He knows that either God is dead or that humanity is now enslaved to an infinitely distant, absolutely alien, and wholly other epiphany of God. To refuse a deity who is a sovereign and alien other, or to will the death of the transcendent Lord, is certainly to risk an ultimate wrath and judgment, a judgment which Christianity has long proclaimed to be damnation. Nor can we pretend that it is no longer possible to envision damnation; the modern artist has surpassed even Dante in envisioning the tortures of the damned. So likewise modern man has known a moral chaos, a vacuous nihilism dissolving every ground of moral judgment, which is unequaled in history. The contemporary Christian who bets that God is dead must do so with a full realization that he may very well be embracing a life-destroying nihilism; or, worse yet, he may simply be submitting to the darker currents of our history, passively allowing himself to be the victim of an all too human horror. No honest contemporary seeker can ever lose sight of the very real possibility that the willing of the death of God is the way to madness, dehumanization, and even to the most totalitarian form of society yet realized in history. Who can doubt that a real passage through the death of God must issue in either an abolition of man or in the birth of a new and transfigured humanity?

The Christian, however, cannot escape the fact that he must make a choice. He must either choose the God who is actually manifest and real in the established form of faith, or he must confess the death of God and give himself to a quest for a whole new form of faith. If he follows the latter course, he will sacrifice an established Christian meaning and morality, abandoning all those moral laws which the Christian Church has sanctioned, and perhaps even negating the possibility of an explicitly Christian moral judgment. Certainly he will be forced to renounce every moral imperative with a transcendent ground, and this means that he must forswear the possibility of an absolute moral law, and at best look upon all forms of moral judgment as penultimate ways which must inevitably act as barriers to the full realization of energy and life. Indeed, the Christian who bets that God is dead must recognize that he himself has not yet passed through the death of God at whatever point he clings to moral law and judgment. True, he can look forward to the promise of total forgiveness, but the forgiveness which he chooses can only be realized here and now; it must evaporate and lose all meaning to the extent that it is sought in a distant future or a transcendent beyond. Yet the Christian who wagers upon the death of God can be freed from the alien power of all moral law, just as he can be liberated from the threat of an external moral judgment, and released from the burden of a transcendent source of guilt. Knowing that his sin is forgiven, such a Christian can cast aside the crutches of guilt and resentment. Only then can he rise and walk.

III. Yes-Saying

Not only has the modern Christian apparently been forced to retreat ever more distantly from the fullness of consciousness and experience, but he has been forced to bear the humiliation of discovering in Oriental mysticism a totality of bliss which is not even partially echoed in the shrinking boundaries of an ecclesiastical form of faith. At the very moment when Christian mysticism is either collapsing or receding behind the walls of the monastic cloister, an originally alien form of mysticism is increasingly becoming real to the Western mind, and is casting its spell upon a contemporary and seemingly post-Christian sensibility. We must note, however, that it has been Western scholarship which has unraveled the depths and subtleties of the Oriental mystical vision; or, at least, it has been Western thinkers who have succeeded in translating the exotic language of Eastern mysticism into the contemporary language of Western experience. When we think of such masters of Oriental mysticism as Mircea Eliade, René Guénon, and Hubert Benoit, we are thinking of uniquely contemporary visionaries, masters who have discovered a new way to the sacred through the labyrinth of our profane darkness. But have we not long since learned that the great poetic visionaries of the modern West have employed a non-Christian mystical language and symbolism as a way to the center of a uniquely modern immanence? One has only to think of the names of Blake, Goethe, Hölderlin, Baudelaire, Mallarmé, Rimbaud, Yeats, Rilke, Proust, and Joyce, to realize that non-Christian and even anti-Christian mystical symbols and motifs can supply a primary source of a symbolic language which is here directed to a total vision of the radical profane. Yet it is Nietzsche's vision of Eternal Recurrence, a vision also employing but inverting the sacred language of the mystics, which most clearly illuminates the thinking and experience of a history which is becoming totally profane.

Few, if any, thinkers have known the sheer horror of existence which Nietzsche unveiled. Casting aside every fixed source of meaning and value, Nietzsche passed through an interior dissolution of an established form of consciousness and selfhood, and resurrected a chaos of meaninglessness lying deeply buried within the psyche of Western man. His quest was not simply a movement toward madness, for he prophetically foresaw the darkness of the contemporary world, a darkness arising in response to the collapse of the foundations of our history. Once the ground of an inherited form of experience has been uprooted, that experience will increasingly become formless, and consciousness will lose both the center and the direction which previously made possible its activity and its self-identity. Nietzsche symbolically employed the name of Zarathustra to distinguish two world epochs of history: believing that the Persian Zarathustra created a moral and religious vision which later became the foundation of Western history, Nietzsche created a new Zarathustra whose prophetic proclamation embodies the end of Western history, an end which that history has reached through its own momentum, and an end which will be followed by the advent of a wholly new historical era. All things whatsoever pass into meaninglessness and chaos when they no longer can be known and experienced from the vantage point of a fixed historical or human ground. But it is only by passing through such a chaos that we can reach the new world lying upon our horizon, a world reversing the forms and structures of our inherited consciousness and experience, and a world promising a new life and freedom to that broken and guilty creature, man.

In its initial form, Nietzsche's vision of Eternal Recurrence records the chaos of a world that has fallen away from its original center. It reflects a totality of perpetual and meaningless flux; no longer is there a beginning or an end, or, for that matter, a purpose or goal of any kind. For to affirm that all things eternally recur, and recur eternally the same, is to grasp an absolutely chaotic movement or flow, a movement in which identity and difference flow into one another, and nothing at all either preserves its own identity or remains different from anything else. Then the world appears as sheer chaos, and existence itself becomes an unimaginable horror. This vision, however, allows us to peer into the abyss, and thus to perceive the ultimate ground of all No-saying: for guilt and resentment are rooted in the interior reality of chaos and emptiness. Yet the new Zarathustra comes to teach a way to the fullness of life in the midst of chaos, to proclaim a Yes-saying which is the antithetical opposite of No-saying, a Yes-saying embodying a total affirmation of meaninglessness and horror. Yes-saying is, of course, a primary symbol of the higher ways of mysticism, always reflecting a final *coincidentia oppositorum,* a total union of transiency and eternity, of suffering and joy. But the classical mystical forms of Yes-saying are interior expressions of the metamorphosis of a profane emptiness and nothingness into a sacred totality, a totality of bliss drawing all things into itself, and thereby negating their original and given form. Zarathustra's Yes-saying dialectically inverts its mystical counterpart, for it embraces and affirms a radically profane nothingness, and does so only by negating the religious quest for a sacred totality.

We shall not understand the Yes-saying of a New Zarathustra unless we realize that it is a total negation of the human and historical world of Christendom, and a negation following from the modern prophet's proclamation of the death of God. With the death of the Christian God, every transcendent ground is removed from all consciousness and experience, and humanity is hurled into a new and absolute immanence. Our chaos becomes manifest as a uniquely modern chaos when it is ever more comprehensively present in response to the emptying of the transcendent realm, as its darkness fills every pocket of light, and night falls throughout the whole gamut of experience. Now an ultimate choice is thrust upon every man, as he can either turn back in horror at our chaos by engaging in a final No-saying, or he can turn forward and meet our darkness by means of an ultimate Yes-saying, a total affirmation of our actual and immediate existence. Such an acceptance and affirmation is possible only if man will give all of the energy which he once directed to a transcendent beyond to the immediate moment, thus releasing every source of energy so as to effect a total engagement with the actual present before him. Zarathustra, and every authentic modern visionary, points the way to a total affirmation of the world, an affirmation which becomes possible only when the world appears as chaos, and man is liberated from every transcendent root and ground. Here, the disappearance of transcendence actualizes a new immanence, as a total Yes-saying to an immediate and actual present transforms transcendence into immanence, and absolute immanence dawns as the final kenotic metamorphosis of Spirit into flesh.

On every side, scholarly critics and theologians point to Nietzsche's vision of Eternal Recurrence as the antithetical opposite of the Christian gospel. Without doubt, this radically profane vision is absolutely opposed to the established dogmas and religious practices of Christianity, so much so that it only becomes manifest and real with the collapse of Christendom. Nevertheless, must the contemporary Christian be forced to confess that a totally immanent existence is wholly other than the life of faith? Will he not then also be bound to concede that the Christian can never fully exist in the world and the flesh? The consequence would follow, of course, that the modern Christian must repudiate that total immanence which has so fully dawned in our world, and stand aside from every contemporary negation of transcendence. Let there be no question about this: to judge Zarathustra as the Antichrist, and Eternal Recurrence as a demonic inversion of the Kingdom of God, is to set oneself against the radical secularity of the modern world, and finally to react with No-saying to the uniquely contemporary history of our time. This is precisely the path of the religious or ecclesiastical Christian today, and we might add that this is also the price which now must be paid for choosing the Christian God. On the other hand, if we can find a way to understand and affirm absolute immanence as a contemporary and kenotic realization of the

Kingdom of God, an expression in our experience of an original movement of Christ from transcendence to immanence, then we can give ourselves to the darkest and most chaotic moments of our world as contemporary ways to the Christ who even now is becoming all in all. Nothing less is demanded of the Christian who would truly and fully live in our world, and nothing less is promised by the radically kenotic way of Christ.

The religious seer and prophet, whether in East or West, initially appears as one who can name the darkness about him, discovering in its dark emptiness a reversal of the sacred, a reversal banishing the sacred far beyond a present or given state of consciousness. Obviously Nietzsche was such a prophet and seer, and like his ancient compeers, his vision is an expression of a prophetic community, beginning from at least the time of Blake and extended into our own day. The modern prophet, however, names our darkness as a darkness issuing from the death of God. Only the seer or prophet who knows the original and all-encompassing power of God can realize the catastrophic consequences of the death of God. Like the reform prophets of the Old Testament or the Taoist prophets of ancient China, the modern prophet can name even our light as darkness because he has been given a vision which abolishes all that humanity has thus far known as light. Both the ancient and the modern prophet must speak against every previous epiphany of light, calling for an absolute reversal of a fallen history as the way to life, with the hope that the destruction or dissolution of an inherited and given history will bring about the victory of a total epiphany of light. Thus we discover in Second Isaiah, the fullest Old Testament prophetic vision of redemption, a call to look forward to the coming transformation of all things:

> Lift up your eyes to the heavens,
>   and look at the earth beneath;
> for the heavens will vanish like smoke,
>   the earth will wear out like a garment,

and they who dwell in it will die like gnats;
but my salvation will be for ever,
and my deliverance will never be ended.
                                        (*Isa.* 51:6.)

The triumphant message of Second Isaiah is inseparable
from a vision of the coming dissolution of all of reality as
man has known it, and it calls for a faith that is wholly
directed to this coming event. A disciple of Second Isaiah
recorded an oracle of the Lord's which most clearly witnesses to this radical prophetic call:

For behold, I create new heavens
    and a new earth;
and the former things shall not be remembered
    or come into mind.   (Ch. 65:17.)

May we take these ancient prophetic words as marking
the very essence of radical faith? If so, when we greet our
chaos with a total Yes-saying, a total engagement with its
dark emptiness, then we too can become open to a new and
total epiphany of light. It is precisely by a radical movement of turning away from all previous forms of light that
we can participate in a new totality of bliss, an absolutely
immanent totality embodying in its immediacy all which
once appeared and was real in the form of transcendence,
and a totality which the Christian must name as the present
and living body of Christ. Indeed, can the Christian accept
those triumphant words in the third part of *Thus Spoke
Zarathustra,* where Zarathustra's animals speak ecstatically
of the redemptive meaning of the symbol of Eternal Recurrence, as a portrait of such a new totality of bliss?

"O Zarathustra," the animals said, "to those who think as
we do, all things themselves are dancing: they come and
offer their hands and laugh and flee—and come back.
Everything goes, everything comes back; eternally rolls the
wheel of being. Everything dies, everything blossoms again;
eternally runs the year of being. Everything breaks, everything is joined anew; eternally the same house of being is

built. Everything parts, everything greets every other thing again; eternally the ring of being remains faithful to it-self. In every Now, being begins; round every Here rolls the sphere There. The center is everywhere. Bent is the path of eternity."

All things will dance when we greet them with affirmation, and then we will be released from the No-saying of guilt and resentment by being freed from all attachment to a distant and transcendent ground. When the path of eternity is bent or curved, then the way down is the way up, and the final or eschatological epiphany of Christ will occur ke-notically in the immediate moment: "Being begins in every Now."

The highest expressions of mysticism also envision a center which is everywhere. But the sacred "center" is an interior depth or a transcendent beyond which reveals itself to be all in all as a consequence of an absolute negation or reversal of the profane, whereas Zarathustra's "center" lies at the very heart of a profane or immanent existence, and it becomes manifest as being everywhere only as the consequence of an absolute negation or re-versal of the sacred. The death of God abolishes tran-scendence, thereby making possible a new and absolute immanence, an immanence freed of every sign of tran-scendence. Once a new humanity is fully liberated from even the memory of transcendence, it will lose all sense of bondage to the past, and with the loss of that bondage it will be freed from all that No-saying which turns us away from the immediacy of an actual and present "Now." Before singing his drunken midnight song in the fourth part of *Thus Spoke Zarathustra,* Zarathustra an-nounces that now his world has become perfect; and he asks:

> Have you ever said Yes to a single joy? O my friends, then you said Yes too to *all* woe. All things are entangled, ensnared, enamored; if ever you wanted one thing twice, if ever you said, "You please me, happiness! Abide, mo-

ment!" then you wanted *all* back. All anew, all eternally, all entangled, ensnared, enamored—oh, then you *loved* the world. Eternal ones, love it eternally and evermore; and to woe too, you say: go, but return! *For all joy wants —eternity.*

Such a love of the world is a total affirmation of an actual and immediate present: but in totally affirming the present, we must will that it recur, and that it recur eternally the same. A refusal to will the eternity of the present, the eternity of this actual present before us, can only proceed out of an attachment to transcendence, a bondage to a power lying outside the present, a power withholding us from a total affirmation of the world. Thus Zarathustra concludes his drunken song of joy with a repudiation of every backward movement to eternity, and an affirmation of the new eternity which is *here* and *now:*

> "Woe implores: Go!
> But all joy wants eternity—
> Wants deep, wants deep eternity."

Can we join Zarathustra in his hymn of praise to joy? Can we, too, repudiate every reversal of the present, every flight from pain, every backward movement to eternity? But this is to ask the Christian if he dares to open himself to the Christ who is fully present, the Christ who has completed a movement from transcendence to immanence, and who is kenotically present in the fullness and the immediacy of the actual moment before us. If a contemporary epiphany of Christ has abolished all images of transcendence, and emptied the transcendent realm, then we can meet that epiphany only by totally embracing the world. Dare we bet that Christ is fully present in the actuality of the present moment? Then we must bet that God is dead, that a backward movement to eternity is a betrayal of Christ, and that a flight from the pain of existence is a refusal of the passion of Christ. The radical Christian calls us into the center of the world, into the heart of the profane, with the announcement that Christ is present here and he is present nowhere else. Once we confess that Christ is fully present in the moment before us, then we can truly love the world, and can embrace even its pain and darkness as an epiphany of the body of Christ. It is precisely by truly loving the world, by fully existing in the immediacy of the present moment, that we will know that Christ is love, and then we shall know that love is a Yes-saying to the totality of existence.

Christian love is an incarnate love, a self-giving to the fullness of the world, an immersion in the actuality of time and the flesh. Therefore our Yes-saying must give us totally to the moment before us, and if we accept its actuality as the "center" which is everywhere, then we can be delivered from every temptation of regressing to a backward movement which is a reversal and diminution of an actual and immediate present. By turning away from the totality of the present, we engage in a regressive movement dissolving the actuality of the immediate moment, thereby disengaging ourselves from the fullness and the finality of existence. In naming Christ as the full embodiment of love, the Christian confesses that Christ is the fullness of time and the world. Christ is the pure actuality of the total moment, a present and immediate moment drawing all energy forward into itself, and negating every backward movement to eternity. Every nostalgic yearning for innocence, all dependence upon a sovereign other, and every attachment to a transcendent beyond, stand here revealed as flights from the world, as assaults upon life and energy, and as reversals of the full embodiment of love. The Christian who chooses the ancient image of Christ as the Son of God, or who is bound to an epiphany of Christ in a long-distant past, must refuse the Christ who is actually present in our flesh. He wagers upon a purely religious image of Christ even at the price of forfeiting the actuality of our time and history. But the radical Christian wagers upon the Christ who is totally profane. He bets upon the Christ who is the totality of the moment before us, the Christ who draws us into the fullness of life and the world. Finally, radical faith calls us to give ourselves totally to the world, to affirm the fullness and the immediacy of the present moment as the life and the energy of Christ. Thus, ultimately the wager of the radical Christian is simply a wager upon the full and actual presence of the Christ who is a totally incarnate love.